INTERPERSONAL COMMUNICATION FOR TECHNICALLY TRAINED MANAGERS

Recent Titles from Quorum Books

Press and Media Access to the Criminal Courtroom
Warren Freedman

Regional Cultures, Managerial Behavior, and Entrepreneurship: An
International Perspective
Joseph W. Weiss, editor

Land Investment and the Predevelopment Process: A Guide for Finance and
Real Estate Professionals
Alan Rabinowitz

Business, Money, and the Rise of Corporate PACs in American Elections
Theodore J. Eismeier and Philip H. Pollock III

Reducing Labor Turnover in Financial Institutions
Presley T. Creery and Katherine W. Creery

Achieving Quality in Financial Service Organizations: How to Identify and
Satisfy Customer Expectations
Robert E. Grasing and Michael H. Hessick

Small Business, Banks, and SBA Loan Guarantees: Subsidizing the Weak or
Bridging a Credit Gap?
Elisabeth Holmes Rhyne

The Corporate Director's Financial Handbook
John P. Fertakis

Motivation and Productivity in Public Sector Human Service Organizations
William T. Martin

Sports Law for Educational Institutions
Steven C. Wade and Robert D. Hay

Public Interest and the Business of Broadcasting: The Broadcast Industry
Looks at Itself
Jon T. Powell and Wally Gair, editors

The Technology Assessment Process: A Strategic Framework for Managing
Technical Innovation
Blake L. White

The Anatomy of Industrial Decline: Productivity, Investment, and Location in
U.S. Manufacturing
John E. Ullmann

INTERPERSONAL COMMUNICATION FOR TECHNICALLY TRAINED MANAGERS

A GUIDE TO SKILLS AND TECHNIQUES

Dale E. Jackson

Q

Quorum Books
New York • Westport, Connecticut • London

Library of Congress Cataloging-in-Publication Data

Jackson, Dale E.
  Interpersonal communication for technically trained managers : a
guide to skills and techniques / Dale E. Jackson.
     p.   cm.
  Includes index.
  ISBN 0–89930–135–5 (lib. bdg. : alk. paper)
  1. Communication in management.   2. Communication in
organizations.   3. Interpersonal communication.   I. Title.
HD30.3.J317   1988
658.4'5—dc19   88–3108

British Library Cataloguing in Publication Data is available.

Library of Congress Catalog Card Number: 88–3108
ISBN: 0–89930–135–5

First published in 1988 by Quorum Books

Greenwood Press, Inc.
88 Post Road West, Westport, Connecticut   06881

Printed in the United States of America

The paper used in this book complies with the
Permanent Paper Standard issued by the National
Information Standards Organization (Z39.48–1984).

10 9 8 7 6 5 4 3 2 1

To my mother, Helen Jackson, who, when I was a boy in Decatur, Illinois, provided me with an early warning system by telling me not to pout and to quit being so sarcastic.

To my wife, Jane, who took over for her.

To our daughter, Susan J. Schweiker, of Leawood, Kansas, and our son, the Rev. Fr. James W. Jackson, of the Blessed Sacrament Church in Wichita, Kansas, whose confidence in me has never wavered.

Contents

Preface

If you have been educated as an engineer, an accountant, a medical doctor, a scientist, a lawyer, or as any other learned professional, then this book is for you. This book assumes you have a professional vocabulary, a store of professional knowledge, and a store of wisdom garnered from your experience. These chapters recognize that much of your current knowledge and wisdom are applicable to the technical aspects of organizations. They also recognize that neither your experience nor your education has prepared you to perform the most difficult part of your career as a manager: interpersonal communication.

This book exists because of the experiences of the author and dozens of his acquaintances when they attempted the transition from the world of a technical profession to that of the people within organizations. While not uniformly bad, those experiences have repeatedly indicated the need for a book to help you, the professional, communicate effectively with those upon whose performance your success as a manager depends. This book is written to present to you an alternative to avoiding confronting someone's performance until a Mount St. Helen's incident demolishes the organizational landscape for miles around.

If you suffer from the habit of backing away from opposition to your ideas when their adoption would have benefitted the firm and you, this book will provide a more constructive alternative. If you find that your communication is primarily directed at satisfying your own ego or that you listen to others either to derive facts or to find an opportunity to take over the conversation, this book will help you become a more comprehensive and more effective listener.

If you see no particular value in observing the unwritten expectations of your associates when you see them for the first time that day or in several days, you will learn some thing about the greeting ritual that will make the rest of your communication much easier. Similarly, if you have no idea of the value and ideal contents of on-the-job small talk (not gossip), adopting these suggestions will benefit your communication when it turns to problem solving. The techniques, mental attitudes, skills, and warnings that appear in these pages are dedicated to an assumption, or you may prefer to call it a principle: "Show me by the way you communicate with me that you see me as capable and important." And having offered the principle in those words, the book has already suffered a partial failure to communicate. The word "important" is misleading. The right word is "lovable." Now to find an answer to a logical question, "If you meant lovable, why didn't you say it in the first place?"

The answer lies in a limitation of the English language and the few definitions but many implications of the word "love." The humanistic admonishment to "Love thy neighbor" first appeared in the writings of Confucius in the fifth century B.C. That commandment achieved supernatural blessing in the Bible and in the Christian gospels. To some, however, love implies something far different—sex. The ancient Greeks avoided that conflict by assigning to sex its own term: "eros." Another implication of the word is the bonds within a family ("filia" to the Greeks). A related interpretation is "liking."

As it is used in this book, the word "love" encompasses none of those. On the contrary, it is intended to imply obligation, benevolence, and compassion, as "Love thy neighbor" did to the ancients. More specific to management, it does not mean that you are a failure if you don't like everyone you work with. It does not mean you are obligated to socialize with your associates off the job or that you have failed if you don't enjoy their company on the job. What it does mean is that when you are in touch with or even thinking about your associates, you have a duty. That duty is to communicate with those persons so as to show them you know they are capable and lovable. The next thirteen chapters are intended to suggest ways of discharging that duty.

This book is addressed to managers, men and women. Except for some of the case studies, however, the pronouns are in the masculine gender. Simplicity won out over s/he and the other combinations often used to avoid an accusation of sexism.

Some Personal Notes

I have wished many times that when I decided I wanted to be a manager, someone would have sat me down and told me to shut up and listen. I wish that person would have given me to understand in no uncertain terms that my communication style and my way of thinking about my associates had to change if I were to succeed as a manager. Further, I wish he had told me that the primary value of having a Ph.D. in inorganic chemistry was when I needed instant acceptance in a collection of others with advanced degrees, and that my being aware of it when I interacted with organizational associates was a serious handicap.

That person never appeared, and that scene never happened. But I did learn, first from a catalytic (see the chemist write?) seminar on active listening and then from years of observing other technically trained managers communicating with their subordinates, peers, and bosses. I learned more about active listening, confronting, and asserting by reading and a lot more by trying, failing, and trying again. The gains are incremental now, but I am still learning and don't intend to stop. I hope you find your catalyst in this book.

Acknowledgments

I would like to acknowledge those many managers and friends whose contributions to my communications have helped lead to this book, but I can't remember all their names. And if I could, this book would be mostly acknowledgments.

In the fall of 1975, Harold B. Ellis, Ph.D., then the Director of Employee Development for Black and Veatch Consulting Engineers in Kansas City, took a chance. Harold agreed I would teach a course on engineering management at his firm. Harold's confidence led to more courses and in them an increasing emphasis on interpersonal communication. Harold was encouraged to take that risk by John M. Amos, Ph.D., then of the Department of Engineering Management at the University of Missouri-Rolla.

Some of the case studies and much of the inspiration to complete this book came from Rebecca Young of Lee's Summit, Missouri. Rebecca was a participant in an early seminar on communication that I led, and we have commiserated many times on the problems technically trained people have with communication.

Eric Valentine of Quorum Books has been demanding yet understanding in his role as executive editor. I look forward to working with him again.

To my co-workers at the DuPont Experimental Station in Wilmington, Delaware, and in the Product Research Department at Butler Manufacturing in Kansas City: I am another case of "too soon old—too late smart."

INTERPERSONAL COMMUNICATION FOR TECHNICALLY TRAINED MANAGERS

1

The Problems Begin, and the Solutions Come from Within

Whether you are a brand new manager or have been at it for several years, you've probably heard that after your first promotion about half of your job is communication. What you may not have heard is that each part of a manger's job has its own set of communication skills.

Before we list those skills, think of your job as having four major parts. One is communicating to help the group of people who report to you meet the needs of the organization or project. Those needs usually include time, cost, and product or service performance. The second part is communicating to meet the needs of the individual members of the group. In the third part, you do things and communicate as an individual to help meet the needs of the project. Lastly, you communicate to meet your needs as an individual.

Now consider your role as a communicator. Before your promotion, you communicated primarily to complement your efforts to meet the needs of the organization and occasionally to meet your own needs. You probably dealt in facts when you discussed the project. Communicating your needs as an individual contributor, however, was another matter. You may never have asked the boss for a raise or objected to the way you were being treated, and in the process you may have learned that avoiding such topics helped your career. On the other hand, you may have protested vigorously that you weren't being paid enough or that your assignment was not what you had expected. Whatever your pattern or communication before your promotion, the more expert you were as a professional, the more likely you continued to rely on professional communication after you were promoted. And that's where trouble started.

This chapter will suggest that your ability to communicate depends not only on how well you know and can apply verbal skills and techniques, but also on how you see yourself in relation to those with whom you communicate. Think of those views as attitudes. This chapter will present those attitudes in the terms of transactional analysis, a branch of psychology, and will call them "ego states." You are already in a kind of communicational incubator, because you have seen two fairly common words combined to generate a new concept. The practice of using familiar words to create new meanings will happen in almost every chapter of this book. The reason for this practice is to create understanding that will lead to your being a better communicator, not a walking dictionary of terms.

Whatever your intention, you communicate very little by words. Most of the messages others derive from you come from your sounds, silences, signs, smells, touches, combinations of these five, and probably by some channels science has yet to identify. This chapter will offer you a means of controlling all of those channels so as to become an effective communicator: one who selects the channels and controls the messages he sends.

This chapter will begin to convince you that the better you become at communication, the more you will realize it is always imperfect.

Lastly, this chapter will introduce the idea that if you want to be fully effective when you communicate with someone else, you have two obligations toward him. First, see him as important. Second, see him as capable. If your attitude toward him is weak on either score, no amount of skill on your part with the language or gestures will allow the two of you to share any understanding. Later in the book, you will use, "lovable," a more effective and more accurate word than "important."

At this point you might conclude that all successful managers have to be psychologists. On the other hand, you may know some psychologists who are in management. You may wonder, if psychology can contribute so much to management, why are its practitioners not better managers? Indeed, some of them are excellent managers, particularly when it comes to analyzing the mental states of those with whom they communicate. Psychologists too, however, have been afflicted with a professional education, its esoteric terminology, and a definition of success that rests on their scientific accomplishments. Their communication with others who are ignorant of the jargon is handicapped.

Appraise the Situation

The size and scope of the problem of communication for technically trained managers can only be approximated, but some data will help. About half the men and women who earn Bachelor of Science degrees in engineering will spend part of their careers in management. To a somewhat lesser extent, the same is true of those who earn degrees in law, mathematics, chemistry, physics, the health sciences, and accounting.

The degrees are intended to produce technical and professional experts. The more expert the person, the more likely that person will be promoted. The more expert the person, the more likely that person will, as a manager, regard subordinates as professional or technical people who are paid to do a good job and should do it. The more professionally competent the manager, the less likely he will be to regard his subordinates as fallible but enhanceable human beings. The more expert the manager, the narrower will be the spectrum of his communication with anyone. The more expert, the greater his dislike of having to write anything.

All these conflicts are complicated by a prejudice on the part of persons with technical or professional education to refuse to accept a boss who hasn't "paid his dues" in the same or a similarly difficult discipline.

None of the material in the preceding paragraphs is encouraging, and some of it explains why engineers and other professionals who are promoted are so heavily criticized by their associates. All of it leaves you with the question, "What can I do about it?"

Part of the answer lies in contributions from psychology, especially from transactional analysis. That discipline suggests that every individual, including you, discovered at a young age that certain patterns of speech and nonverbal communication resulted in parental approval. Other forms did not. The successful forms are those that signaled obedience, cooperation, and generally "being a good boy." The successful forms were modified or reinforced in school and perhaps in military service.

By the time you earn your college degree and take a job, further modification of those forms is extremely difficult. The reason for the difficulty is that modification involves not only learning new combinations of words and gestures, but also changing mental attitudes toward yourself and others.

Set the Objectives

The stage has been set; now what can you do? The answer is to learn first to manage yourself before you try to manage others. Learning self-management means you learn communication skills and the mental states that go with them. Whether you have just begun the transition to management or have been at it for a long time, you can learn and you can change. Prove that to yourself, and you will never stop learning.

Select the Effective Mental State: Back to Transactional Analysis

Transactional analysis is a theory of human communication. It has several components, one of which is ego states. Those states have names: *parent*, *adult*, and *child*. It may sound as if the words are intended to convey the age or maturity of the persons involved in a communication. Rarely so. Instead, think of the words as abstractions for the roles in which you see yourself and the role (usually one) you expect the other person to adopt when you send a message to him.

To illustrate the concept, assume you are in a phone conversation with a subordinate. If part of what is on your mind is that you are the boss, your speech or your tone of voice will convey it. That means your mental state will control some, and maybe most, of what you say. In more specific terms, if what you say in this conversation and how you say it are replays of your experiences with your parents, teachers, and bosses, you are communicating from your *parent* state. Still more specifically, if you see yourself as the judge who metes out punishment or as the order-giver or as the critic, you are communicating from your *critical-parent* state. If you see your job as the guidance counselor, the back-up rescuer, or Big Daddy, you are communicating from your *nurturing-parent* state.

Think of the critical-parent and the nurturing-parent states as all that you learned about how people who are older and have more authority communicate with those who are subordinate to them. You learned by observing your parents and other adults. You learned communication patterns that were intended to cause you to obey. You learned some patterns that were intended to reward you for obeying and others that parents used when you did not obey.

You learned there was usually a payoff if you did more than just obey. If you complemented your obedience with a smile or pleasant words, you may have been rewarded with praise or affection. You were communicating from your *adaptive-child* state in a way that those in power liked and saw as positive. Your world was a better place for a while.

You probably also learned a host of other ways to cope with parental authority—some of them viewed by parents as negative. In *Leader Effectiveness Training* (p. 15) Thomas Gordon lists fourteen such coping behaviors, including total submission, withdrawing into silence, and outright rebellion. Here is one place where the name of the ego state from which you communicate coincides with the label parents (or bosses or associates) apply to you. They say, "He is acting like a child," or "He is being childish." When someone refers to you in that way, he means you are communicating from your adaptive-child state, and he sees it as negative.

When you were young, you were the object of communications that stressed rights and wrongs and dos and don'ts. Inevitably, you became aware of inconsistencies between what adults in their critical-parent roles told you to do and what they did themselves.

At school, you received messages from teachers and coaches. Many of those messages came from the speaker's critical-parent state. Some came from his nurturing-parent state. Either way, you learned how to cope with what he said by communicating from your adaptive-child state. You found a job and almost immediately saw that your boss usually communicated from his critical-parent or nurturing-parent state. If your adaptive-child communications to the boss primarily emphasized positive aspects, your career progressed.

Some time early in life, you learned to communicate from another part of your *child* ego state: the *natural child*. This is the part of us that lets loose with emotions—all of them. It is spontaneous, honest, and part of what makes us human. Unfortunately, most mothers and fathers are selective in which natural-child communications they tolerate. Boys soon learn it is okay to communicate their happiness but not their sadness: "Big boys don't cry." Girls usually don't hear that message and thus develop a much broader range of communications from their natural-child state. Most managers try to avoid communications from the natural child and do not welcome them from subordinates.

Fortunately for those organizations that value creativity and whose profits come from inventions, the *child* ego state has another compartment: the *little professor*. When your communications are aimed at expressing new, untested ways to design an electrical circuit or run a chemical reaction, your little-professor ego is active. He does not accept traditional wisdom about science or interpersonal communication and is forever trying something different. If those tries are made in the chemical laboratory and subject to reasonable precautions, they can result in invention. From invention may come a patent and then increased profit.

The little professor is equally at home, however, in contributing imagination to the adaptive child as it copes with authority. An apocryphal story from a troop ship during World War II in an Atlantic crossing can illustrate the little professor at his worst. An officer insisted upon inspecting the bunks of the enlisted men very carefully. The bottom bunk was so close to the deck that it was impossible for the soldiers to clean under it thoroughly. The officer, nevertheless, continually reached underneath, found dirt, and assessed a penalty. After a few such experiences, someone's little-professor ego saw a potential in the double-edged razor blades common in those days. Somehow several of those razor blades were broken in half the long way and wedged into the seams of the deck under the bottom bunk. After one encounter between bare hand and razor blades, the officer decided to forego that part of the inspection.

When you are communicating logic, rationality, and avoiding pre-determined judgments or pre-made decisions, you are in your *adult* ego state. This state has a valuable function: it is a switching mechanism that decides unemotionally from which ego state to send the next communication. Describing communications that come from the adult ego state is easy. Finding managers who communicate frequently from it is not.

You send messages from all of these ego states. Moreover, it is impossible to send those messages using words or numbers alone. There is always a variation in tone of voice, facial expression, or a dozen other nonverbals (see Chapter 6).

There is no ideal ego state for the technical manager. There is, however, an ideal combination of states. That combination includes primarily the adult, natural child, little professor, and, once in a while, the *nurturing-parent* ego states. In more conventional terms, the manager is more effective when he can either communicate from the adult state or use it as a logical switching device to select a more appropriate ego state. The value of the natural-child state is in having a sense of humor that will allow the manager a good laugh at his own expense. The little-professor state pays off because the benefits of creativity are not limited to the chemical laboratory. In fact, the benefits of using the little-professor state can accrue under the rational and logical regime of a formal, problem-solving/decisionmaking discipline. The manager can rely on the creativity of the little-professor state when trying to identify the cause of a problem. In Kepner and Tregoe's decision analysis, creativity is invaluable in generating alternative courses of action.

The nurturing-parent state is for those cases in which, at least for a short time, the manager's most effective course of action is to shore up a subordinate whose own skills are insufficient to the task.

The critical-parent role is most favored by managers and least favored by their subordinates. It is seldom adopted by conscious, logical choice, being more a product of habit or of watching other managers. It can appear to be working, as long as its transmissions are directed toward and reflected by the adaptive-child state of the subordinate. For the two of them to continue to communicate effectively, the subordinate must play the role of the obedient adaptive child. The most damaging aspect of such a communication process is that it confirms the beliefs of both parties. The manager has evidence that progress comes from being the authority. The subordinate is convinced that the only way to survive is to go along with him.

Choose the Skills to Attain the Objectives

I borrowed from Kent Thoeni, of Allied-Signal in Kansas City, a list of habits he recommends to those who wish to be successful in business.

One of those habits is, "Seek to understand before you seek to be understood." Chapter 4 will enlarge on that habit as it pertains to the values of listening. At this point, it is a light that can guide your innermost thinking when you are trying to communicate with someone else.

Here's another guide. In *Hamlet*, Shakespeare had Polonius give some advice to his son Laertes that is at least as good today as it was in Denmark in the Middle Ages. The advice was, "Above all, to thine own self be true." Chapter 5 will enlarge upon that admonition. For now, let it be your foundation as you start to think about honesty in your communication.

If you like to construct models to help you examine systems, create one to help you understand interpersonal communication. If you like flow charts, here are some suggestions about what to put in a flow chart on communication.

1. Include a sender who is under the influence, if not complete control, of an operating system (ego state).

2. Give that sender several sets of equipment, each of which has a signal source, an encoder, and a transmitter.

3. Mark one of those sets, "Words." (When you read Chapter 6, review your model and decide how many nonverbal communication sets you want in it.)

4. In any event, make sure you put at least one filter and at least one source of interference in the path of every transmitter.

5. Add a person who will be the receiver and has a decoder and a device to detect both verbal and nonverbal signals.

6. Make sure the receiver has at least one filter and at least one source of interference for each kind of incoming signal.

7. Provide for the possibility, but not the certainty, of some kind of response from the receiver to the sender.

8. Omit any control center upon which you can rely to hook up the right transmitters and receivers or to avoid problems caused by filters and interference.

By now, if you haven't given up on this whole idea of communication because of all the problems you can see with your model, you are ready to learn.

Avoid the Risks Inherent with the Skills

You probably know someone who seems to select the right ego state and transmission content without apparent effort. You may wonder if that person came by this skill naturally. Perhaps so, but as you become more proficient in the techniques of communication, you may find that the skills do not come naturally. They have to be learned.

Whatever you do, don't conclude that you can always understand someone with whom you communicate according to your model or this book. You are a manager, not a psychoanalyst. Even if you are a psychotherapist, and even if you have attained the heights Carl Rogers did, you are sure to find that there are times when, try as you may, the skills are either out of your reach or seem to be ineffective. So what do you do when that happens? One answer is to take a break and try again later. Another answer is to write, or at least talk about, the thoughts that concern you. What you write can help you see what ego state you are in, where you are not being true to yourself, or where you are not seeking to understand before you seek to be understood. This "self-disclosure" process will lead you to a solution more quickly if you do it in the presence of another person—particularly one who can listen carefully and without passing judgment.

If the study of interpersonal communications is new to you, even though management is not, don't expect to convert to the status of skilled practitioner in a few months. In fact, you will probably still be converting on the day you retire. Think of yourself as somewhat like Sisyphus, who, in Greek mythology, rolled a heavy stone up a mountain. The stone always rolled back down, but you, from time to time, will reach the top. When you get there, take a few minutes to look back and see where and how often you slipped. The next trip will be easier.

The Rewards

Emerson said it best: "The reward for a thing well done is to have done it." When Bob Lemon was reminded of all the publicity he received during his major league pitching career, his comment was, "All those newspapers have been used to wrap the trash." Sure, it's nice to hear the praise, and it's nice to get a raise. It's even nicer to get the promotion you wanted. Sooner or later, however, all those things become like the newspaper wrappings. No one but you will appreciate how hard you tried to share your embarrassment for not having tried hard enough.

Someday you may find someone who is really good at listening, and perhaps that person will help you express your own pleasures and regrets about your ability to communicate. If you are that fortunate and have already encountered someone who seeks first to understand, realize how rare that person is. Speakers are many; open-minded listeners are few.

Another reward is that you may become what Carl Rogers described as a "fully functioning person." In the process, you can also become a well-rounded manager, capable of communicating effectively in the most trying situations. You will appreciate the values of patience, persistence, and perseverance. You will appreciate the values of forgetting about yourself in an effort to ensure good communication with someone else.

Assign your own estimate of worth to it, but I suggest that the most significant reward from a career point of view is to blend the best of your professional and managerial skills. Start with your professional degree and all the mental acuity it took you to obtain it. To that technical strength, add the communication skills essential to a successful manager and a set of mental states necessary to support those skills.

Fit the Skills to Yourself and Your Job

Carl Rogers told us how hard it was for him to learn to be open to his experience. For the technical manager that means learning to sense the environment in which you operate and especially to sense the pressures that can interfere with your ability to communicate.

When you see anything in this book, or in another other book, that you feel might be useful to you in communication, compare it to the way the successful managers in your organization communicate. You will find much you want to change, but take your time. Look for models who will give you clues to the words, tone of voice, and gestures most likely to help you gain acceptance of the changes you seek.

There is also the question of timing. You may find that to make significant progress you need only to say the right words at the right time. That means, before you start sending signals, think for a moment about who is present and what pressures are on that person. Too much pressure on someone will mean little, if any, receptiveness to your suggestions.

Patience Gains Acceptance by Associates

Whatever you do, don't go back to work having read part of this book or having gone to a seminar on interpersonal communications and make any announcements about what you're going to do about it, except observe the ways the managers communicate. Further, don't go back to work and start using any of the terms you read here. In fact, don't do anything differently for several weeks. Then, reread the book, write down the things that concern you, and draw up a plan for practicing what you think the book is trying to teach. The important thing is to make your changes in communication fit the situation. If you employ a technique you have learned and someone else recognizes it, sees how effective it is, and calls it by its textbook name, you have both made progress. You can the agree that, yes, you were trying to do exactly that.

On the other hand, don't be surprised if the other person says something like, "Well, I think it's a lot of bull." Corporate halls are filled with people who have been burned because someone had only a partial grasp of the mental conditioning necessary to be a good communicator. This book was not intended to call other people's attention to you. On the contrary, it is intended to call your attention to how you communicate, the skills of effective communication, and how to use them.

A Problem Solved

DM, an engineer, was promoted to department manager. He brought three things with him to the new job: a tremendous talent in mechanical design, his microcomputer, and a tendency to talk about the job and very little else. For a while, everything went nearly perfectly. DM was in the position to use his talents without the interference of the person to whom he had reported. He found that his designs attracted more attention from upper management than ever. He also found that he could improve the designs of his former erstwhile peers, now his subordinates.

Primarily because of the mistakes some of his subordinates made, he came to regard them as having limited competence, needing his constant attention and frequently his criticism. Hand-in-hand with the criticism went more use of his microcomputer and less time communicating with his subordinates, along with less time communicating with his boss. It wasn't long before DM's subordinates started complaining, and their complaints reached DM's boss. The complaints went something like this: "He seldom talks to us, and when he does, it's to tell us what we've done wrong. We know he's one of the best in the business at what he does as an engineer, but he seems to think he's paid to find something wrong in what we have done. Not only does he insist on checking everything, but he is always telling us we are behind schedule."

The first time DM's boss heard all this, he dismissed it as another example of promoting a good engineer and obtaining a less-than-perfect manager. When it became obvious to him that the schedule was slipping and the new manager was as much a subject of gossip as of respect or admiration, he knew the next move was his. He set up a meeting with DM one afternoon and arranged that they would not be interrupted. After they had talked a while, he realized that DM was under considerable pressure. DM wanted to apologize for the fact that a couple of his projects were behind schedule, and his boss heard him out. Then the boss asked DM what he thought the company expected of him as a department manager. The answer was quick: to get the job done on time, within specifications, and under budget. It was at this point that DM's boss realized DM had a long way to go in professional development.

Inasmuch as the problems at hand seemed to be more those of communication than of a lack of technical skill, DM's boss took a big pad of white paper and sketched a diagram that was essentially four axes. There were the usual X and Y axes, and two Z axes: one that projected into the plane of the paper, and one that projected out from it. DM's boss explained that the XY coordinates came from some writings by Robert Blake and Jane S. Mouton, and that the X axis was the one to which most newly appointed managers paid the most attention. The X axes represented the things a manager does to make it more likely that the group would finish the project on time, within specifications, and within budget. The communication skills necessary for success along that axis meant that the manager had to transmit his wishes as clearly as possible and then obtain feedback from subordinates to make sure they understood what they were expected to accomplish. DM's boss took a few minutes to explain ego states and then described the communication requirements of the X axis as being primarily that of the adult ego, which logically and unemotionally transmits directions to and receives information from the members of the group. It also involves the nurturing-parent ego, which occasionally has to teach or fill in for the still-developing skills of a subordinate. When a project is completed properly, there is a place for the natural-child ego to enjoy the result and celebrate!

The Y axis is a different matter. It involves saying and doing the things that help the subordinates realize that their boss sees them as human beings and is concerned about their welfare. The ego states required for this skill are similar to those along the X axis, but the manager strives to minimize the amount of time spent in the parent role and stays mainly in the adult role.

Communication between the manager and the unit members along the Y axis is entirely different from that along the X. Here, the skills of listening (Chapter 4) are paramount. The listening may take a lot of time. The information the manager receives while listening may seem to be trivial, but it is nonetheless important for the manager to "hear out" the unit members. In fact, if communication along the Y axis is improper or incomplete, the effects will be negative along both the X and the Y axes. Along the Y, there will be deterioration of more subtle measures, such as being late for work, frequent requests for transfers, too-long lunch breaks, and too much time spent in idle chatter.

The negative results along the X axis are more easily measured. They amount to failures to meet schedules and specifications.

It was at this point in the discussion that DM interrupted his boss to point out that if all engineers just did their jobs, these problems wouldn't even exist. DM's boss had to agree, to a point. That led him to define the Z axis. He described the Z axis that projects into the plane of the paper as representing the professional abilities and accomplishments of a manager: in this case, his engineering designs. The boss said he realized it was futile, and in most cases unwise, to ask an engineer or other professional to abandon his professional background as part of a promotion. The problem, however, is that the engineer-turned-manager can feel so comfortable doing technical jobs that the X and Y axes are almost forgotten. In such cases, the new manager does so much of the engineering that the he is carrying two briefcases home at night and complaining about the lack of productivity of his subordinates.

The ego state most appropriate for communication along the Z axis is the adult. The most useful content of communication along the X axis is facts. Problems arise when the Z axis that projects into the plane of the paper becomes so dominant that it excludes or minimizes the amount of time the manager spends communicating along, particularly, the Y axis.

The other Z axis is one about which most men would rather not talk. The Z axis that protrudes from the plane of the paper describes the things the manager does to meet his own needs. Many of those needs are psychological, which means that the manager's natural-child ego state may be the source of messages (Chapter 5). Most managers whose backgrounds are strongly technical or professional are not aware of how to communicate along this part of the Z axis, or the value of that communication; so they avoid it entirely. This is unfortunate, because it is the part of a manager's communication that makes him seem human.

DM's boss took a half-hour to explain all this, and then both of them were silent. DM finally spoke up, saying something like, "Why didn't they tell me?" He thanked his boss for putting things in a way he could understand and for giving him a model against which he might chart his progress.

They adjourned with two agreements. One was that they would get together in a couple of weeks to see how things were going. The other was that his communications had a long way to go.

References

Blake, Robert, and Jane S. Mouton. *The New Managerial Grid*. Gulf, Houston, 1978.

Emerson, Ralph W. "New England Reformers," in Charles W. Eliot, ed., *Essays and English Traits by R.W. Emerson*. The Harvard Classics. P.F. Collier, New York, 1909.

Gordon, Thomas. *Leader Effectiveness Training*. Bantam, New York, 1980.

James, Muriel, and Dorothy Jongeward. *Born to Win*. Addison-Wesley, New York, 1971.

Kepner, Charles H., and Benjamin B. Tregoe. *The New Rational Manager*. Kepner-Tregoe, Princeton, New Jersey, 1981.

Miller, Donald B. *Working with People*. CBI, Boston, 1979.

Rogers, Carl R. *On Becoming a Person*. Houghton Mifflin, Boston, 1961.

Thoeni, A. Kent. Personal communication, Kansas City, Missouri, September 1986.

2

Little Ridges Lead to a Mountain

This chapter contains a model to help you understand where you have been, where you are, and where you might be going in a communication process involving at least one other person. You will also learn something more about transactional analysis (TA) in this chapter. More specifically, you will learn how people structure communication time and which ego states and kinds of transmissions are appropriate for each structure.

Appraise the Situation

Let's start with the definition of time structuring. Communicating time is structured in six ways. Each structure is characterized by the nature of the strokes exchanged and the ego states from which they arise. (A *stroke* is any kind of signal sent by one person to another. If the second person responds with any indication of having been stimulated by [having received] the stroke, the two have completed a *transaction*.)

The simplest form of the time structuring involves no strokes. Call it *withdrawal*. In such a structure you are usually alone and not exchanging strokes with anyone. Hermits and members of religious orders have come to appreciate the value of the contemplation that can occur during withdrawal. Its values extend to the business community. For example, a few years ago, transcendental meditation (TM) became popular in executive suites. TM involves repeating a simple sound (your personal *mantra*) while mentally separating yourself from the outside world. TM is said to result in significant reduction of mental stress and accompanying physiological strains.

During most of the working day, however, withdrawal is impractical.

Instead, humans are almost forced to communicate. The following model may help you understand some of the aspects of that communication.

First, think of yourself and the person with whom you are communicating each walking along a ridge toward a mountain. The ridge has a rounded top and gently sloping sides. Now imagine you have just seen each other and you both have been indoctrinated in the proper forms of greeting. You both say things like, "Hello," "How are you?" "OK," and, "See you later." The "How are you?" is not a request for a recent medical history, and the "OK" is not a report on vital signs. This collection of strokes is the second form of time structuring, called *ritual*. The words of ritual vary widely. Such variation may require you to revise ritual when becoming acquainted with someone new. However the two of you work it out, as long as everything goes according to the routine, each of you stays on your ridge and proceeds either to an encounter with someone else or to the next phase of time structuring.

If either of you violate the routine, however, the other is likely to leave the rounded top of the ridge and start sliding down one of the slopes. Think of moving down the slope to the left as an instinctive tendency to fight, or at least become aggressive. Your instincts may send you down the right slope. On it, you reduce further contact with this person. Taken to its extreme, you may actually leave the scene (flight). In flight, you restrict your communication to the point of entering withdrawal. You may feel an obligation to remain present physically, but constructive communication with the other person becomes almost impossible.

Because of these alternatives, the model needs a few more representations of the risks involved in interpersonal communication. First, add a wind that comes in gusts and gains strength as the altitude of the ridge increases and its sides become steeper. Think of that wind as your instinctive reaction to threatening or stressful messages sent to you by others. Second, add a surface that becomes slippery as the altitude increases. Think of that slipperiness as your still-developing knowledge of which mental attitudes will be far more important than words in the difficult situations that can occur in critical emotional or factual conversations.

Whatever the reasons, the technical professional often fails to observe even the barest requirements of the greeting ritual. I remember being unpleasantly surprised in graduate school by that failure. I would meet a fellow student, and everything would go well. A few days later in the hall of the chemistry building, however, I would pass that student, say "Hello," and receive only a slight nod, or nothing, not even eye contact, in return. My first reaction would be to search my memory for what I might have done wrong. When my search proved fruitless, I would be left with a feeling of mild resentment toward the offender and a resolve to get even by ignoring him.

Many years later I was leading a group of secretaries, filing clerks, and technicians in a discussion of the greeting ritual. I casually observed that most people had learned to observe the ritual and that the real problems were with listening and other more exotic subjects. I was wrong. This group soon convinced me that the biggest improvement their company could make in communication would be for the engineers just to say, "Hello," look a secretary in the eye, smile, and say her name.

Now back to the model. If you find yourself in trouble, consider your alternatives. You can stay in either fight or flight until someone else appears who is skilled enough at listening to allow you to climb gracefully back onto the ridge. But those listeners are rare. You can also apply the skills in Chapter 3 and substitute one or more of the techniques of assertiveness for either aggression or retreat. Or you can apply the skills in Chapter 4 and assume the role of the listener. Whichever alternative you choose, your job is to assume an ego state that will allow you to regain the ridge without driving the other person off his.

Now that you know some of the negative aspects of the model, assume the greeting ritual went well and that you and the other person want to communicate on matters of greater gravity. Because of your technical background, you are probably about to make a serious error; you want to get to work. Don't. Instead, prepare to enter a third form of time structuring, in which the strokes are more intense. This form is usually called *pastimes*, but you may think of it as small talk or chit-chat. (*Pastimes* is discussed in more detail under "Choose the Skills to Attain the Objectives.") For now, realize that the slopes on either side of the ridge are steeper, the wind gusts are more frequent, and the broad surface of the ridge is narrowing. In other words, the risks are greater.

Pastimes means taking time for what may appear to have no organizational payoff to inquire about such things as the other person's family, automobile, thoughts on an impending sports event, or opinion of the latest income tax legislation. The strokes in pastimes are more significant. Pay more attention to their content, and you will learn more about the other person than you did in ritual.

Listen carefully, even if you aren't interested. You can learn something from everyone with whom you speak. Sometimes you will learn new terms or new meanings of old words. You will establish yourself as an interested, caring person and a good conversationalist, even if you say very little. You will have the opportunity to listen without having to evaluate the speaker or the words. Pastimes is most effective when all parties are agreeing, but you can disagree with what the speaker says without making it personal. By now, you will have realized that pastimes is an art that takes patience and much practice.

Technical groups are seldom comfortable in pastimes, so you can count on them to get down to business within a few minutes. (If they appear reluctant to leave pastimes, be prepared for trouble later. It may mean they see something coming they would rather avoid.) In TA talk, getting down to business is called *activities*. Technical managers like to call it "problem-solving" or "decisionmaking." Whatever the label, managers are paid for making decisions. The problem they face, however, is that staying on top of the mountain requires careful and often delicate communication. Activities means first that it is time to talk out the emotional problems and then move into the factual or innovative aspects.

When both the emotional and the factual problems have been solved, the clouds around the mountain part to disclose a peak. In TA, that peak is called *intimacy*, or *authenticity*. If you prefer, call it *trust*. It is rare—so rare that many people never experience it. In any event, it does not last long.

Now, while you have been moving from pastimes to activities, the ridge has led you onto the mountain. The surface has iced over, and a fall down either the fight or flight side would be disastrous.

Inside the mountain is a hidden cave, where the managing engineer can store resentment and thoughts about retaliation. One tunnel in the cave leads to the flight side of the mountain; another leads to the fight side. The cave and the tunnel to the fight side provide immediate refuge for those who choose to avoid outright combat, but whose resentment occasionally sneaks out as sarcasm.

The cave exists because many organizations place a premium upon cool, unemotional communication. Managers who let their emotions guide their speech either do not progress in management or are quickly (and privately) corrected. Those managers usually adjust their behavior to attain the organizational norm. Then, although they may have the same reactions to unpleasant situations, they learn to store those reactions in the cave. As a result, they risk sudden, uncontrolled emotional explosions, with negative effects upon the firm, their careers, and their health.

Now think of the ridge and the mountain both sitting in an enormous catchbasin. Call the catchbasin *games*. It is the sixth and last part of time structuring. This catchbasin is where the put-downs, the zingers that issue from the cave, and the rest of the negatives strokes go. Dr. Dru Scott, in a training film, "Transactional Analysis," claims that games account for over half of the communication in organizations. Here's an example of games in action:

A manager's son had always found math to be a problem. His grades had been generally low and neither he nor his father were happy with the situation. The father was an engineer, which meant his skill in math was far above that of most of us. He had tried to help his son and was overjoyed one evening to hear his son report that he had earned a "91" on his last math test. Without even thinking, the father asked, "What happened to the other nine points?" The accompanying deflation stayed with his son for a long time.

The mountain is a model of communication under stress. The left, fight, side has two sections. One is most appropriately called "roller derby." That term also comes from Dru Scott's film. It seems a group of managers agreed that sport most closely approximated what went on in their organization.

The other part of the fight side is total destruction. Here ancient history provides an example in the third Punic War. Rome had beaten Carthage in the first two Punic Wars, and Carthage was down, but not out. The conflicts were decimating the Roman ranks, and so, when they won the third round, they burned Carthage, knocked down the walls that still stood, and sowed the ground with salt so that nothing would ever grow there again.

The lessons? Stay on top of the mountain if at all possible, but if you do choose to come down on the fight side, don't stop at roller derby; go to Punic War III. That means you must have a provable cause, be within the terminate-at-will law, and have the personal courage to remove someone from the organization.

Set the Objectives

Now that you can visualize the time structures, how can you, the engineering manager, learn effective communication? One way is to practice saying "Hello" and "How are you?" using first names, and responding to others who say the same until you are familiar with, if not entirely comfortable in, the greetings ritual. Generally, this means to practice such communications until you feel more at home with casual conversation that does not involve technical or economic facts.

Another worthwhile objective is to learn to listen and contribute to casual conversation (pastimes). Later you can become familiar with the techniques of assertion (Chapter 3), listening (Chapter 4), and confrontation (Chapter 5), and use them to stay on top of the mountain during the activities phase.

Lastly, learn to avoid the trap of exchanging the negative strokes that characterize games.

Select the Effective Mental State

The nurturing-parent state is ideal for the greeting ritual. It is particularly valuable when the other person responds to your question, "How are you?" with a lengthy discourse.

Small talk is the time to agree. That means staying in the parent state and addressing others as if they were in it too. This is one of the few times when you and other people can be in your critical-parent roles and agree on such things as how poorly the government is handling some current economic problem. The secret is to avoid addressing the other person's child ego in the form of a criticism.

In problem-solving, the trick is to identify and overcome the feelings before taking on the facts, whether the feelings are yours or someone else's. The methods for overcoming these feelings have been described in dozens of books and articles, but none of the methods is easy. As M. Scott Peck states in *The Road Less Traveled*, life is hard. Moreover, the successful methods are more than combinations of words. They accommodate the mental states that are essential to using those combinations successfully over a long period.

Choose the Skills to Obtain the Objectives

Although it is not the therapeutic, emotion-exploring listening covered in Chapter 4, listening during greetings and small talk is a fine art in its own right. It involves inviting the speaker to speculate on the implications of something that seems to interest him. It involves listening for a cue, after which you may insert some thought of your own that complements one of the speaker's. Small talk means being not just politely interested in the speaker's conversation, but genuinely so, even if it is not your field. It means asking questions to explore someone else's interests. It means complimenting someone on the grasp of a subject, his accomplishments, or some constructive attitude he may display. Being comfortable in small talk means being aware of current events and being ready to express an opinion, but not one that is likely to be controversial.

If the occasion is purely social, this means staying in small talk for the entire evening. It means overcoming your own boredom. It means overlooking someone else's inability to express himself clearly or to organize his thoughts. It is not a time for confidentiality, which is sufficient reason to avoid or limit the intake of alcohol.

If the occasion is a business function and you are in charge, switch from small talk to activities when you think everyone has had a chance to contribute. Most of your colleagues will not be comfortable with small talk. Be prepared, therefore, for signals that they are bored.

Avoid the Risks Inherent with the Skills

Small talk is not a time to participate in gossip. Gossip is tempting, but will boomerang. Any contribution you make to gossip will probably be incorrectly repeated and exaggerated. It is not a time to address the other person's child ego state. That means don't criticize, don't blame, don't accuse, don't imply, and don't give orders.

Don't sell and don't try to solve problems. You may be asked for suggestions about a serious problem. If the other person appears to be serious, make an appointment for later. Don't be surprised, though, if the need has evaporated when you meet the other person again. Don't counsel. That means, don't reflect anyone else's emotions, and don't express any emotions of your own.

Inevitably you will encounter in small talk people whose speech will lead you to form an opinion of them. Opinions can lead to labels, and labels are trouble. Labels are abstractions; they are usually incomplete and are unfair to the other person. A more practical danger is that labels can do your thinking for you and lead you to inaccurate conclusions about someone's value as an engineer or manager. Avoid them.

Although Addeo and Burger's *EgoSpeak* is unfortunately out of print, the authors made a lasting contribution to the risks of engaging in small talk. The authors proposed that everyone has an insecurity reflex that is stimulated by the presence of someone who makes him feel inferior, and that each of us tries to overcome the inferiority through our conversation by making fun of others, bragging, or making suggestive remarks. In those situations, the person speaks from the adaptive-child state and tries to make the little boy in himself feel more like an adult.

The lesson that Addeo and Burger tried to teach is not to allow someone else's misuse of small talk arouse your insecurity reflexes. Small talk is not an excuse for one-upmanship.

The Rewards

Small talk can be an invaluable source of leads to significant information without, however, supplying the information itself. Ritual and small talk can help other people learn to trust you. Don't underestimate the value of people starting to see you as someone who is interested in them as persons, rather than just as members of a project team. Spend a few minutes with a word processor operator, or someone new with the organization, and exchange views about the weather or something that might interest that person. Your investment can be invaluable when you later ask that person to do something on your behalf that is above and beyond the call of normal duty. The biggest payoff from doing a good job in ritual and pastimes at the start of a group meeting is that everyone is usually ready for activities. A secondary benefit is that emotional conflicts may be partially alleviated. Moreover, it is less likely they will revert to pastimes later in the meeting.

Fit the Skills to Yourself and Your Job

The next time you chair a meeting, pick out a topic with which every-one is familiar and deliberately allow the group to spend some time reinforcing each other's opinions. In most cases, the group will grow impatient with the small talk and will signal their readiness to go to work. Meanwhile, you can assess the psychological climate for the day.

As the leader, don't let your conversation regress to small talk after the problem-solving has started. If you see the group is trying to get back into small talk, or if you feel strongly that you would like to do the same, it is likely there is a problem the group simply does not want to confront. Chapter 5 deals with confrontation and offers several sug-gestions as to how you can effectively cope with an unproductive group meeting.

Patience Gains Acceptance by Associates

The first time you try to install small talk as a developmental step in a group problem-solving situation, be prepared for impatience. It may only be that people are not comfortable unless they are doing work they feel is constructive or speaking in familiar ways. If they are aware that you have become a student of communication, their suspicions of your motives will increase. The answer is for you to be patient. Weather the objections and continue to make small talk a part of any group meeting. Most importantly, let your associates see by your example that you are comfortable with whatever they may wish to include in small talk and that you welcome the opportunity to talk about things that interest them.

A Problem Solved

Here is a partly hypothetical instance of the way Sam, an engineering manager, had to learn how to say "Hello." Sam admitted he may never have learned some finer but more important parts of communication, had it not been for a suggestion list and a car pool.

Sam thought he said "Hello," or something like it, as often as the next guy. Because of that assumption, he was shocked when he read the suggestion list assembled by a consultant at a recent seminar his organization had held on supervisory responsibilities. When the lecture was about over, the consultant arranged the class into small groups and asked each group to write at least one thing that would improve com-munications in the plant. Sam found one group had suggested every-body should say "Hello," and he thought the idea was trivial. He realized people ought to speak to each other when they meet, but primarily if they had a problem on which they needed to cooperate. On the other hand, Sam knew people in the company who would stretch a "Hello" into a ten-minute conversation, if given the chance.

Sam didn't care a lot for this ritual because of something that had happened to him in school. He had said "Hello" to one of the faculty members in what he thought was a perfectly friendly way, but the response had been an obscene gesture, not the return greeting Sam had expected. After that, Sam issued his greetings sparingly.

Sam would have forgotten about the suggestion list if he'd not had an opportunity to talk with one of the older operators. That operator had also been at the seminar and heard the suggestion about saying "Hello." The operator said he had lost count of how many times he had spoken to some engineer or scientist in the hall and had received, at best, a monosyllable reply. What he said made Sam realize that the operator had come to think that being ignored was par for the course with technical people, especially because the operator didn't have his engineering degree. The operator pointed out that you don't really have to say anything. You can wave your hand. You can smile or even roll your eyes. The more Sam thought about this, the more he realized how much he liked to hear his name spoken by someone else and to have it accompanied by a smile or at least said in a pleasant tone of voice. Sam also came to realize that almost everyone likes that same thing.

Sam's learning was helped by an experience in his car pool. Sam and the driver were talking in the car when the second rider climbed in without saying a word, and pretty soon conversation died. Sam later saw the driver, during coffee break. The driver was still trying to find out what he had done wrong or what was wrong with the second rider. He admitted he had been worried all morning about the incident.

How the two of them worked it out, Sam never knew, but the effect on him was profound. Everyone expects a "Hello," or something like it, and if he doesn't get it, he is likely to spend a lot of time wondering what is wrong.

Cross-References within This Book

Chapter 4 offers help when the other person falls off the mountain. Chapter 5 offers help to the manager when he is about to fall. Chapter 6 is a look at the nonverbal communication that accompanies our messages, whether we are on the ridge or on the mountain.

Chapter 7 covers the communication of facts, which is what most managers see as the primary aspect of their jobs. One of the goals of this book is to convince you that factual communication is something you will do much better after you have learned to stay on top of the mountain by first solving the emotional problems.

References

Addeo, Edmund G., and Robert E. Burger. *EgoSpeak*. Chilton, Radnor, Pennsylvania, 1973.

James, Muriel, and Dorothy Jongeward. *Born to Win*. Addison-Wesley, New York, 1971.

Peck, M. Scott. *The Road Less Traveled*. Walker & Co., New York, 1985.

"Transactional Analysis." Organizational Development File Series, CRM Educational Films, DelMar, California, 1975.

3

Being Assertive Means Staying on Top of the Mountain

Part of what you will learn from this chapter is a set of techniques—eight of them, to be exact. But more importantly, you will learn what assertive communication is and which of your ego states are most effective in being assertive. In a more general sense, you can expect to learn how to use your adult, rather than your adaptive-child ego state.

Appraise the Situation

When you were a kid, you learned to deal with parents and other bigger people who punished you. Psychologists call it "coping." You may have cried, run away, vowed revenge, refused to cooperate, broken things, alibied, lied, and sometimes even obeyed without question. Whatever you did was even easier to do the next time. You found ways to justify that behavior, particularly that which helped you avoid some of the punishment.

Being obedient, especially when coupled with working hard, sounds ideal. In an environment where frequent and specific praise is given for such behavior, it is ideal. B. F. Skinner called that praise "positive reinforcement." Unfortunately, B. F. Skinner's ideas on positive reinforcement have been adopted by only a few organizations. The result? Being obedient avoids punishment, but it doesn't help you develop as a manager or communicator.

The situation is even bleaker when you remember what Dru Scott said about 55 percent of communication in organizations being games. When you think of games as giving negative strokes or doing things that earn you negatives from someone else, you can see why assertive techniques and an assertive mindset are so often the subject of seminars. The objectives include rescuing people from the games habit.

If you look up "assert" in the dictionary, you will find the following definitions:

1. To maintain as a right or claim, as by words or by force.
2. To insist on the recognition of oneself.
3. To state positively, to affirm, to allege, to aver, to declare.

On the other hand, "assert" connotes the idea of controversy, which differentiates it from "affirm," "state," and "tell." The *Oxford Universal Dictionary* reports that "assert" first appeared in 1604 and later came to mean "to set free." The last definition is rare, but indirectly implies the principal value of being assertive.

Being assertive does not mean being passive, nor does it mean being aggressive. Although one of the synonyms for "assertive" is "aggressive," the techniques you will learn from this chapter involve staying on the mountaintop from Chapter 2. That top has no room for passivity or aggression.

Here are some other synonyms for "assertive" that may help you think of it as a state of mind, or part of a philosophy for regarding other people: determined, positive, exploratory, receptive, observant, emotionally neutral, stable, equitable, accommodating, natural, dependable, polite. Assertion is truth that, while not always completely expressed, will give you freedom.

Set the Objectives

The objectives of assertive communication spring from these definitions, with the additional element of an external source of stress, which may arise from any of several sources. It may come from someone who is trying to dissuade you from a position you know is right or from someone who is into games. It may come from your need to reach at least a temporary agreement with someone you find it hard to deal with. Whatever the cause of the stress, the broad objective of being assertive is to maintain your personal and organizational rights without negatively affecting someone else's rights in the process.

A more specific objective is to learn to receive criticism objectively. Criticism sent in your direction is really aimed at something you did or said or failed to do. It is the act that merits the criticism, not you.

Another objective is for you to realize you don't have to be assertive in every situation involving communication under stress. You may elect to withdraw by saying nothing. You may elect to be aggressive, or at least to seem aggressive by raising your voice.

Lastly, this chapter is intended to teach you to have an objective for using an assertive technique before you use it.

Select the Effective Mental State

Being assertive demands that you "keep your cool." Your ego state is that of the adult with enough of the nurturing-parent state to have and show respect for the position of the other party. You recognize the source of communications that issue from another person's critical-parent state, but you respond from your adult state and communicate what is logical and reasonable. You state positively that which can be stated positively, and you feel no obligation to say more. Anything else, and you will be communicating from your natural-child, adaptive-child, or critical-parent state.

In terms of the model, you will slide down the mountain and into either fight or flight. You may find yourself on the fight side, being the aggressive child or the critical parent. You may become the natural-child and start an argument, or you may become the adaptive child and hide in the cave, waiting for a chance to get even and taking with you a load of resentment.

You have the right to expect adult-to-adult criticism of your errors. That means criticism that concentrates on the error, not the person. Unfortunately, most of those with whom you associate will either not know how to communicate from the adult state or will not be able to avoid using their critical-parent state.

Choose the Skills to Attain the Objectives

The literature on assertion is best exemplified by Manual J. Smith's *When I Say No, I Feel Guilty*. In it he emphasizes how to avoid feeling worse when you take an unpopular position or making things worse when someone attacks you or your actions. Smith's advice is flexible enough to be useful whether or not such attacks are justified.

Smith suggests how you can hold a position and resist all attempts to cause you to change your mind. He calls it "broken record." *Broken record* means that you calmly state your position and, when you encounter objection, you restate your position. You don't apologize for your position, nor are you rude. Broken record further means that you continue the process until either the other party accepts your position or the two of you strike a balance. Mastering broken record will allow you to feel comfortable while you ignore the other party's attempts to manipulate you, needle you into becoming emotional, or apply irrelevant logic to the situation. Broken record is as useful to you when you have control over the situation as when you do not.

Used alone, however, broken record not only has little value, but it can generate aggressive behavior on the part of the other person. For that reason, don't use it unless you first give verbal recognition of the other party's position. Smith calls that verbal recognition *fogging*. When used to precede broken record, fogging includes such statements as, "I can see that you feel that way," or "I'm sure this is important to you." Don't worry about choosing the best set of words. What you are trying to do is to let the other party know you respect his right to have a point of view, even though you don't agree with it.

You may prefer the words "acknowledging" or "recognizing" to describe this technique. No matter which word you use, it is much less important than your belief that the other party does have a right to his own position.

Acknowledging, or fogging, has an even more useful application independent of broken record. Consider a case in which you have been accused of some failure, but you know the accusation is inaccurate. If you communicate from your critical-parent ego state, you will probably find something to criticize in the performance of your critic. If you allow your child state to taken over, the result may be a trip to the cave, outright aggressive speech, or total collapse. Again, let your adult state come to the rescue. Here are some phrases you might use.

1. "You may be right."
2. "I guess you could think that."
3. "I'll have to think about that one."
4. "I'll take that under advisement." (As if you were a judge on the bench.)
5. "That's a point well taken."

Remember: You are only admitting the other person has a right to speak to the subject. You are not challenging the content of what the other person said, and you are not attributing accuracy to an inaccurate criticism in the interests of maintaining harmony.

Whatever you think the motivation of the critic might be, keep in mind that further exploration of the topic is to your advantage. Should that happen, convert the criticism to one of three kinds of questions, and state those questions in a way that is acceptable to the critic and useful to you. When you use this technique to explore a less-than-obvious cause of a problem, start your question with the word "why." If you want to choose a course of action, start with the word "how." If you want to anticipate and control damage from the unexpected, start with "what if." Label the technique *manageable concerns*, as termed in chapter 7 of Kepner and Tregoe's *The New Rational Manager*.

For example, let's say you are in front of a group and that its members have certain dissatisfactions with the way you or your group is treating them. More specifically, they think you have been taking too long to process their expense accounts. They have few specifics, just gripes. Keeping in mind that you can learn more from an unhappy client than a satisfied one, you are ready to convert their dissatisfaction to a manageable concern. Think about what they are saying for a second or two and then ask for their concurrence to restate the problem as, "How can we convert your expense sheets into checks more promptly?" You choose that statement because you know that your people can do a better job of being sure that the check requests are all written before the end of the day. You also know that those who are doing the complaining can fill out the expense forms more accurately and turn them in more promptly. Rather than criticize their performance or defend your own, you have proposed an objective that can be attained by better performance on both sides. You have proposed a means of "managing their concerns."

The difference between manageable concerns and acknowledging is the ego states of the parties to the communication. In acknowledging, you are in the adult mode and are trying to avoid further problems with the other person's child or critical-parent mode. In manageable concerns, you are inviting the other person's adult ego to join you in exploring a problem situation. You may find that the invitation goes unaccepted. If so, be patient. Many of the persons with whom you communicate either have poorly developed adult ego states or have them carefully hidden under a load of parent and child camouflage.

What about those instances where indeed you were in error, and the critic has announced it for all to hear? What is your instinct? Is it to forego rational analysis and to dredge up something in which the critic was in error? Is it to deny the facts or their implications? Or is it to launch into an extended apology, followed by a promise not to do it again?

Don't do any of those things. Instead, practice what Smith calls *negative assertion*. You are not obliged to make a quick reply. Instead, think about the facts of the situation and put together a reply that has two parts. The first part is simple enough: It is to admit the error. The second is more complicated and is best described, again by Smith, as *self-disclosure*.

Suppose you are accused in a meeting of having failed to include a vital part of a set of performance specifications. Use words like these: "You're right; I blew it [that's negative assertion], and I feel like an idiot for having caused other people so much trouble [that's *self-disclosure*]." You might wonder why those words did not contain an apology, especially if you were taught to apologize when you caused someone a problem. Apologies have their benefits, but they also place a burden on the injured part to accept or deny them. Best course of action? If you are asked for an apology, give it. If you deliberately did something to cause injury, then apologize. Otherwise, let the self-disclosure of your embarrassment suffice.

Suppose part of the accusation is true, and part is not. In that case, deal only with the true part. Admit the mistake and say how you feel about having made it. Then wait to see what the critic does next. If he is determined to cause you additional embarrassment, repeat the admission of error and the self-disclosure. Eventually the critic will grind to a halt. At that point you may assume most of the vitriol is gone and it is safe for you to propose a plan to avoid such errors in the future. If you have no such plan but you think that having one would be a good idea, you can state your intent to develop a plan and let it go at that.

One of the advantages of admitting mistakes while in the adult state is that it allows you to realize the mistake was a fault in one of your actions and no more than that. It was not indicative of all of your many other actions, nor of you as a person.

Consider a situation in which you have proposed a certain action and someone else, without apparent logic, criticizes the action you have in mind. It's time for what Manuel Smith calls *negative inquiry*. The idea is to ask specific questions to explore the depth and nature of the critic's position. You don't even have to present your inquiry as a question. For instance, you could say something like, "I don't understand what is so bad about that idea." More effectively, preface negative inquiry with negative assertion. For example, use words such as, "You're right, I did do that, but I don't see the problem," and then wait to see if the critic is willing to go further. This technique requires a fair amount of patience on your part, and it is based on the assumption that the critic, for one reason or another, has not said what is really bothering him. Therefore, it's up to you to keep him talking until you get to the basis of his objection. For negative inquiry to succeed, it requires that you maintain an open, receptive mental attitude and that your nonverbal signals transmit an interest in hearing what the critic has to say.

Assertive techniques also include *free information*, for the times when the best thing you can do is listen. Chapter 4 will discuss listening in detail. For now, however, consider the rewards of relying more on your ears and eyes than your vocal cords when the other person is "wound up" about something. The cause for all the talk may have been something that you were associated with or it may just be that you were convenient. Let's say that your firm is trying to install a "client-centered" philosophy for dealing with suppliers, customers, and fellow employees. You have just run into a person whom you seldom see and have made a comment about the new program. What follows is a mixture of invective, self-pity, and some potentially damaging factual information.

Chapter 4 will teach you how to use a very specific form of listening ("active"). Now, however, see this conversation as a means of learning. For the new philosophy to have a chance of succeeding it will need universal acceptance. You are now in the presence of an employee whose support will be needed, who has some severe reservations, and who is disclosing all that to you. The other person's comments may not be well organized, and his conclusions may be too sweeping. But forget all the faults of his discourse, listen to him! The information is "free" except for the few minutes it takes you to hear him out. Bypass your impulses, however well-justified, to point out the weaknesses in his position or to debate with him. Instead, listen and you may be led to some ways to make the client-centered idea work even better.

Another way to be assertive is to use the technique of self-disclosure. Chapter 5 will deal with self-disclosure relative to confrontation. Meanwhile, you can use such simple disclosures as, "I don't know," when asked a question to which those present seem to expect you to know the answer.

There is one more technique for assertion. Smith calls it *workable compromise* and offers it as a means of resolving stand-offs. Consider a situation in which everyone present has used broken record and the attempts at manipulation and criticism have all been made and resolved, but the technical or economic needs of the parties to the discussion have not been met. It is time for you to suggest a compromise. The objective of workable compromise is to "split the loaf" without worrying about which side gets how much of that loaf. The objective does not include being fair, and the result may be no more than a truce. It does mean, however, that you and the other party both agree to live with the compromise. It also means no one leaves the scene with a feeling of having been short-changed.

Labor-management negotiations are often an exercise in negotiation leading to compromise, but it isn't always workable. Consider a case in which management insisted on the right to change the work rules to allow engineers to participate physically in the assembly of prototypes without the shop steward filing a grievance. The union representatives agreed to the change but only after gaining an increase in dental benefits. When the representatives reported to the membership, however, the contract was voted down because the operators in the prototype model shop thought the proposed change was unfair to them.

Another bargaining session failed because the head negotiator for management insisted on obtaining a concession from the union for every concession given by management. His position was that any agreement must be fair and to be fair it had to be as close to 50/50 as possible.

Had both the union and management representatives come to the table with certain minimum objectives that were fully supported by their constituents and without any preconceptions of what was fair, they might have avoided a long strike.

Avoid the Risks Inherent in the Skills

If not preceded by acknowledging, broken record can be infuriating. Even if it is properly prefaced, broken record may lead to having your own way, but at someone else's expense. A warning from Samuel Butler applies: "He that complies against his will is of his own opinion still." Remain alert for any indication of disappointment or helpless acceptance by the other party. If you detect either, summarize the agreement and invite the other party to express misgivings. Convert them to manageable concerns (how, why, or what if) and renegotiate.

Acknowledging is a disarming and normally useful route to avoiding unjust criticism. If, however, a contractual relationship exists between your firm and that of the critic, even the slightest admission of the possibility the critic is correct could be very expensive. In such cases a noncommittal reply, such as, "I'll have to think about that for while," offers the benefits of acknowledging, but without its risks.

Acknowledging has one more problem. Suppose your boss was present when you were inaccurately accused of having made an error. You used acknowledging, but the boss either was not fully aware of or was not certain of the facts. Meet with your boss at your earliest opportunity and make sure he has the facts. Acknowledging will show him you are capable of keeping your head under fire. Your giving him the facts will assure him you know your job.

Negative assertion, like any other technique, has a potential weakness. If you are unable to maintain communication from your adult ego state, even if you use exactly the words this and other books recommend, your nonverbal communication may ruin everything. If, for instance, your tone of voice could be interpreted as flippant, an onlooker may easily conclude that not only did you make the mistake but you are personally not concerned with its consequences.

Negative inquiry can be excellent for getting to the source of an objection. It carries three risks. One is that your style of questioning will become that of the critical parent. Having been addressed in that manner, the objector is more likely to be guided by his emotions than by your interest in learning the factual basis of his objection. A second risk is that negative inquiry is a confrontation, insofar as it places a demand on the other person. Stay away from "you" or "your," and stay away from questions. Instead, use clauses like, "I don't understand." The remaining risk of negative inquiry is that as your skills in using it increase, it takes on some aspects of therapy. The objector comes to trust you and may reveal some basis of his objection that you would just as soon not have heard at all.

Self-disclosure of emotions, for all its value, may be out of place in an organization where the majority of men takes pride in not revealing their feelings. Most men were told when they were young, "Big boys don't cry." The Spartans of ancient Greece saw feelings (except anger) as equaling weakness, and they did not want to be weak. Like the Spartans, men in most environments are uncomfortable with the revelation of their feelings or those of any other men.

This is one of the few places in the practice of assertion where women have an advantage. They are usually not brought up to see the expression of emotions as a weakness and, therefore, find self-disclosure in a managerial situation as both useful and normal. But a caution: Displaying emotion in most male-dominated organizations is acceptable and effective only when the emotion is anger. Fortunately, the pendulum is swinging toward a broader acceptance of the expression of emotion by both men and women. Nevertheless, such expressions are effective only when they relate to on-the-job performance.

Workable compromise may be all you can accomplish in certain business situations. But here's a warning: If the deal won't fly when you get back to your group or to your boss, the compromise is not right, no matter how good it looked to you. Another warning: Don't confuse compromise with cooperation. It may be the basis for cooperation that comes later, but at the time it is agreed to, it is no more than a truce.

If all these risks were the only ones associated with assertion, it would qualify as the most useful technique of communication known to our species. Unfortunately, our culture has imposed upon it a handicap. More specifically, the same words and nonverbal signals accepted and even admired in a man will often elicit a different reaction when a woman uses them. If she uses broken record, no matter how skillfully, she may be labeled a "pushy broad," or worse. If she is too quick to use self-disclosure of her emotions, having been accused publicly of an error, she may be condemned for acting like a woman, rather than like a manager who knows how to communicate in difficult situations.

Ethics also have a role in assertion. Martin and Schinzinger, in *Ethics in Engineering*, speak at length of ethics based on the rights of those who use the products of engineers. The authors also discourse on the duty-based ethics of those whose special knowledge allows them to design structures and products to be used by the public. Engineers who have been promoted into management have an ethical duty to communicate in ways that enhance the lives and careers of their associates. Those who work with engineers in management have an ethics-based right to expect such communication.

The Rewards

The toughest lesson to learn about assertion is how to communicate from your adult ego state under externally applied stress. Having done so, however, you can navigate the roughest of waters in project reviews, client briefings, and other meetings, whether one-on-one or with a group. You can come out of those meetings with something of value to you and to those who report to you without having made interpersonal relationships worse between you and others present. You can express yourself on the most sensitive topics without being dependent on the affections of others.

Assertion can give you a means of avoiding the impact of someone's aggressive, negative messages on your objective. It allows you to communicate on important topics, however sensitive, without being dependent on the good will of others.

If you do all these things without ever mentioning any skills or the word "assertive," your boss and others who work with you will learn to count on you to negotiate difficult situations logically and without becoming emotional or starting arguments. More specifically, your use of negative inquiry will often lead to the discovery that your critic was speaking from a misconception. If you have used that skill to provide a drain for any obstructive emotional aspects from the critic, you are then in an ideal position to apply the facts and the logic that will clear up the detail. The application of logic would have been totally useless had you tried it when you first heard the criticism. On a more mundane note, negative inquiry can overcome your failure to hear or to decode correctly the other party's criticism.

In addition to making you more effective in your communications as a manager, your learned reliance on the adult ego state offers a corollary benefit that has nothing to do with communication. Spending time in the adult state and asserting yourself in difficult situations are excellent ways to avoid building up your internal stress levels. You learn to separate emotion-based criticism from the facts as you know them and to let your communication concentrate on those facts, not on the personalities. Let's suppose that in your environment all communication is in carefully modulated tones. Everything appears to run smoothly, and top management makes it clear they expect "civilized behavior." Although you may feel like raising your voice, especially after you have been inaccurately accused of having made a mistake, let your adult state take over. Keep your voice low and your manner calm.

If, on the other hand, loud speech and even shouting are frequent, do what you can to match the volume used by those who criticize or debate with you. Your being loud, in this case, is not a product of your emotions. Your adult state decides that you are in Rome, so you do what the Romans do. On the other hand, don't try to imitate someone in the organization who is always articulate and who seems to have a store of carefully honed and appropriate verbal expressions. To be assertive is to be free of imitation. Develop your own vocabulary.

Using manageable concerns to reconcile the objections of others with your own purposes is almost sure to succeed. If you are in an action-oriented organization, rather than one based on inquiry, avoid questions that start with "why" and concentrate on "how." But be prepared for a future problem. Managers who resist dealing with questions that ask "why" will often arrive at decisions in answer to "how" questions that have little chance of working because they did not first explore the underlying cause of the problem.

Be particularly careful about converting someone's objection to a "what if" question. Prophets of gloom are seldom popular. If, however, over time you are eventually able to encourage other managers in the organization to think more carefully about how they follow up on decisions, "what if" examinations of what might go wrong with those decisions can become a valuable part of the communication process.

More generally speaking, the value of being assertive derives in either very negative or very constructive situations. If the other party is into games, assertion endows your communication with a mental state and techniques that tend to bridge the gap between you. If both of you are in the activities or authenticity parts of time structuring, assertion provides you with the techniques for complimenting and expressing your regard for the other person's position.

Fit the Skills to Yourself and Your Job

Women who practice being assertive are seen as pushy, so if you are a woman and don't like that adjective, what do you do? One alternative is to let it go by and keep on with the assertion. If that isn't consistent with the way you would like to be regarded, put yourself on video and enlist an objective critic. Ask that critic what your body movements and facial expressions and tone of voice convey. Do they suggest someone free of the frustrations of having to be "like a man" or having to play the role of the domestic or the sex object? If that freedom isn't there, get busy. It's time to be assertive.

Remain in your adult ego state and don't change your language or nonverbals just because you are using the skills of assertion. Profanity and obscene gestures in a stressful situation are more fitting from your child state, not your adult. So, too, is the practice of introducing the things most important to you with anything that may sound like an apology. If you believe it, state it positively in a tone of voice and with the eye contact that match your conviction.

Your parent state is equally out of place. Even if your male colleague is acting like the spoiled brat, don't get into your parent state; stay in your adult state. Don't "talk down."

In a discussion start firmly and assertively and allow yourself the privilege of backing off. Don't start softly reserving aggressive speech for later, when you encounter opposition. If you aren't sure where to employ what you've learned about assertion, switch to free information for a while and be prepared to use broken record when it's time to establish your position.

If you do run into emotional opposition, it's time for active listening (see Chapter 4) until the other party has stated his position more logically. Then you can use workable compromise. Do that a few times and the "pushy broad" will have been replaced by the colleague who "knows what she wants."

Patience Gains Acceptance by Associates

Your use of the adult ego state, in spite of its being essential to assertion, does not provide a quick means of convincing others of its value. Your best chance is to influence others by your own example. You will know your patience has been rewarded when someone recognizes some technique you used in a particularly troublesome meeting and later compliments you on how well you used it. It doesn't matter that they don't know the correct name for the technique or that they never heard of ego states. What does matter is that your actions have helped them see the light.

Consulting engineering and architectural firms are often advised to survey their clients about the firm's image. The results are often a surprise and always useful in planning a campaign for more business.

Your communication pattern also has an image. Before you prescribe which of the skills of assertion (or of the other communication domains) you want to develop, do enough research among your associates to find out how they regard your communications. The first step? Do a situation appraisal as outlined in Chapter 10. Such an appraisal will cause you to interview some vitally important people, such as your boss, but don't leave out your peers, your subordinates, your secretary, and representatives of various groups in the organizations with which you interact.

Situation appraisal can lead you to problem analysis (see Chapter 10) via concerns stated as questions starting with "why." If a "why" question turns out to be top priority for your communication, keep in mind that you are seeking a change that may have resulted in a distinction in your communication. That distinction is either causing problems or is partly responsible for your success.

Managers are seldom patient enough to seek the answer to why something is wrong. They want to know what to do about it. If that habit fits you, the next step is decision analysis. It starts with your setting a series of objectives, classifying them into *musts* that can be measured or *wants* that can be weighted, and coming up with actions that seem likely to do the job. Out of all this comes a plan of action that includes possible adverse consequences and a secondary plan for overcoming their effects. Since your objectives will have to do with assertiveness (or the lack of it) in your communication, your decision analysis means planning to change, and scheduling checkpoints with those who were part of your original "image" research.

If you are a woman, one of the objectives in your decision analysis may be to change men's reactions to your being assertive. It is possible, but only if those men see your being assertive as working to their advantage. One of your "must" objectives will be to demonstrate that you are using assertion to advance the organization's goals in addition to your own.

Start the process with a confession. Tell one of the men that you want to bring your assertive abilities to an effective level, but you are concerned about the effects on your male associates. Ask him to take the role of the objective critic and tell you how he reacts to the ways you communicate. Be prepared for some resistance; men don't disclose themselves easily. You may have to communicate from your obedient adaptive-child state, and, by your questions and attention, encourage the man to communicate from his nurturing-parent state. One result of sessions like this will be discovering some ways of looking at the musts and the weights of some of the wants you had not considered. Another result will be a new viewpoint on the possible adverse consequences.

The obvious difficulties in making such a change may tempt you to see the masculine reaction to your assertiveness as unmanageable. That may be the most productive decision. But don't let it be simply an easy way out that perpetuates a situation that benefits neither you nor the organization.

Problems for You to Solve

"That's the last damn time I'll suggest anything to him."

My name is David. I've been a supervisor in this outfit for almost seven years and have been on top of my job all the way. I've found that things go best for me when I think through what I want very carefully, check it out with another engineering supervisor, and then present it. I don't like having to sell my ideas. If the company had followed up on some of my ideas, we would have a much better operation.

The reason we aren't better, as I see it, lies in the stubborn refusal of some of the management to listen to good suggestions. In fact, I'm beginning to think some of them are being deliberately obstinate. Maybe they want to test us. I don't know.

Just recently I came up with a way to help our microprocessor development. I thought about it for several days before I told another supervisor, and she thought it was pretty good. Then I took it to the boss. He listened okay, but then he started talking about something remotely like my idea that someone had suggested a few years ago that didn't work. It was clear he wasn't interested in my idea. After listening to him ramble for a while, I walked out. I've had it with taking ideas to him. In fact, I think I'll just do my job from now on.

"The guy never stops needling."

I was promoted from plant engineering to supervisor about a year ago, and I'm still learning how to handle some of the people in this outfit. For instance, my name is JoAnn, and I think it is a pretty neat name. Trouble is, we have a guy in this outfit who thinks he is hot __ when it comes to needling other people. He told me my name sounds like it belongs to a Barbie doll.

When he tries that kind of stuff with some of the other supervisors they either tell him off or ignore him. But I have to admit that he really gets under my skin. I guess I wouldn't mind that kind of thing if I didn't know he likes to accuse me of making some simple mistake and then needling me about it in front of my boss.

I blew up in one of those situations because I knew I was in the right. The boss told me later that the company expected its supervisors to hold their tempers, no matter what the circumstances. That's okay for the boss to say, but he doesn't have to deal with this jerk every day.

"I hate like hell to get caught having made a mistake."

My name is Don. I have been a supervising engineer here for almost ten years. You'd think I would have learned how to act when the boss points out to me that I've made a mistake. In spite of the time I've put in on this job, it still embarrasses the hell out of me when the boss, or anyone, for that matter, tells me I've done something wrong. My instinctive reaction is either to find an alibi or try to minimize the bad effects of what I've done.

The thing that really bothers me is when the boss goes on and on about it. I usually end up by apologizing and asking if there's anything I can do to help the situation. I usually feel pretty low for a day or two after one of these instances. I'm looking for advice from someone who has been in supervision or management for a few years.

"After we have had one of these fights, I never know how to leave things."

People call me Mac, most of the time. I have been a project engineer in the structural department for several years, and my job is not getting any easier. The job wouldn't be bad if I didn't have to spend half my life arguing with those jokers in SCX.

Sometimes the disagreements start as pretty minor things, and then they get blown all out of proportion. Other times they start big and end bigger. In neither case do we seem to get down to the core of the problem or really try to work it out.

I have learned that the only way to come out alive is to yell louder than the other guy and make damn sure I don't come out with the short end of the stick.

I understand some of the management think I'm a real bully, but I notice they really like it when I boot one of the projects home on time and within budget. This whole thing stinks.

Problems Solved

"That's the last damn time I'll suggest anything to her."

David may never become the world's best salesman, but his career will develop faster if he substitutes his dislike for having to sell his ideas with the adult-based realization that some form of persuasion of his boss and others is essential for his designs to be given fair consideration, no matter how technically superior those designs may be. In terms of the techniques of assertion, David has a better chance of his boss accepting his ideas if he will learn how to combine acknowledging with broken record and simply stick to his guns. He may want to use negative inquiry when his boss starts bringing up things that were tried several years ago and didn't work.

"The guy never stops needling."

Acknowledging was virtually created for JoAnn and others like her. The more she reacts emotionally to the guy who needles her about her name or inaccurately accuses her of making mistakes, the more he's going to needle. She is in an environment where managers are expected to hold their tempers. If JoAnn tries to return the needling, it will prolong the process and probably make things worse. If, however, she says something to the effect that perhaps her name does sound as if it belongs on a doll and keeps that up as long as the needler wanted to play his little game, he would soon realize it wasn't working and transfer his attentions to someone else. When he says something about her having made a mistake and she knows he is wrong, her best bet is to acknowledge the accusation, but neither admit it nor deny it.

"I hate like hell to get caught having made a mistake."

If Don will learn how to use negative assertion and couple it with self-disclosure, he will soon realize that mistakes are not more than that. Everyone makes them. Most of them can be overcome, and minimizing or alibiing are a waste of time. The apology may be okay, if Don's boss says he wants one. A better practice would be to think through and then propose a plan to overcome the effects of the mistake.

"After we have one of these fights, I never know how to leave things."

Mac likes to fight. He is a sitting duck for someone who likes to needle or for someone who likes to point out other people's mistakes. Mac can benefit by using all of the techniques of assertion, particularly manageable concerns and workable compromise. He could ask an otherwise hostile group to state their problems and then seek solutions. That part of his determination that lets him bring projects home on time and within budget will not be injured, and may even be enhanced, by his learning how to use the techniques of assertion.

References

Alberti, Robert E., and Michael L. Emmons. *Your Perfect Right*, 3rd ed. Impact, San Luis Obispo, California, 1978.

Butler, Samuel, in Bartlett, John, *Familiar Quotations*. 14th ed. Little, Brown & Co., Boston, 1968, p. 353.

Kepner, Charles H., and Benjamin B. Tregoe. *The New Rational Manager*. Kipner-Tregoe, Princeton, New Jersey, 1981.

Martin, Mike W., and Roland Schinzinger. *Ethics in Engineering*. McGraw-Hill, New York, 1983.

Oxford Universal Dictionary, 3rd ed. Oxford University Press, London, 1964.

Skinner, B.F. *Beyond Freedom and Dignity*. Bantam/Vintage, New York, 1972.

Smith, Manuel J. *When I Say No, I Feel Guilty*. Bantam, New York, 1975.

Taetzsch, Lyn, and Eileen Benson. *Taking Charge on the Job*. Executive Enterprises, New York, 1978.

Weisinger, Hendrie, and Norman Lobsenz. *Nobody's Perfect*. Stratford, Los Angeles, 1981.

Zuker, Elaina. *Mastering Assertiveness Skills*. AMACOM, New York, 1983.

4

One Part of the Mountain Is Active Listening

"I know you believe you understood what you think I said, but I'm not sure you realize that what you heard is not what I meant."

This chapter is to help you learn how to listen according to the needs of the other person. You will learn what active listening is, how to be an effective active listener, and the differences between listening for facts and listening for feelings. More specifically, you will learn where active listening fits into a technical or business conversation and where it does not fit. You will learn how to solve some of the problems active listeners encounter, and to reduce the risk of having such problems. You will see how active listening helps you remember more of what you see and hear during communication with someone who is under stress. Last, and probably most important, you will learn the value of setting aside, if only temporarily, your own concerns and stresses in the interest of helping someone else talk out his concerns.

Appraise the Situation

A good part of the type of listening that fits so well under small talk is listener centered. Unlike the listening that was appropriate to small talk, active listening is centered on the other person. Think of it as unselfish listening.

As you read the rest of this chapter, you will see that active listening is a skill you need most when you least want to use it. More specifically, it is a skill and a frame of mind to use when the other person either does not accept your position or seems to be in the grip of his emotions.

Those emotions can be negative, such as frustration or anger; they can also be positive, such as relief or happiness.

You will also see in this chapter the reason for its advocacy of your learning to be good at active listening. Suppose you know about two hundred people in a professional sense. Ask yourself if this fits them:

> Most people are convinced they are valued only for what they can contribute to the project, the organization, or the boss's career. They derived that idea from being cut off rather than listened to by authority figures for most of their lives.

If that does fit with your experience, you will realize that most managers fail entirely to recognize the importance of their associates as human beings, and they usually fall short in recognizing the capabilities of those associates. You will also realize why this chapter is so important for managers.

Set the Objectives

In the broadest sense, there are two guidelines for effective interpersonal communication: (1) Show me by your communication with me that you recognize I am lovable, and (2) Show me you recognize that I am capable. The importance of one individual is usually considered to be less than that of the group. In fact, Dr. Joseph Fletcher, in his *Situation Ethics*, proposed an ethical standard for our decisions involving others as "doing the most good for the greatest number of people." On the other hand, the scriptures tell us of a shepherd who risked the safety of the flock to rescue a lost sheep. Dr. Fletcher's guiding principle was, "Love thy neighbor." It doesn't always give us a clear picture of the most loving course of action, but it does set a standard that applies to the manager-subordinate relationship.

That choice isn't easy, and seldom do we have to make it. Active listening, however, offers a means of recognizing the importance of an individual, and usually without loss to the group.

Active listening first requires you to prepare yourself to accept any message of any kind from another party without passing judgment on either the person or what he says. Further, prepare yourself to try to understand the other person's point of view, no matter how far it may depart from reality as you understand it.

When active listening is used by a psychotherapist, the objective is the improvement of the client's mental health. When practiced by a manager, the objective is a productive, effective relationship between listener and speaker.

Select the Effective Mental State

Seek first to understand, and then to be understood. Both disagreeing with someone and being in the presence of someone who is displaying emotion put pressure on you. Rather than trying to understand the other person's position, it is so much easier and more familiar to dictate, threaten, appeal to a sense of duty, apply labels, interrogate, or change the subject. You may also try to give advice, insist on sole reliance on facts, play the amateur psychoanalyst, or try to cheer up the other person. None of those approaches can overcome disagreement or help someone else through emotional stress, nor do any of them recognize the basic capabilities and importance of the other person.

Active listening, in contrast, requires you to be in your logical, rational, adult ego state, whether the other person is in his emotional child state or has the rigid, closed mind of the critical parent. As much as you may be tempted to move into your critical-parent or nurturing-parent state, don't. Stay in your adult.

The foundation of active listening is that it is a means of helping other people solve their problems, particularly those that involve emotions. That helping action is most effective when you try to see things the way they do. Call that activity *empathy*.

Your helping role is even more effective when you can maintain an unconditional positive regard for the other person. That does not mean you have to like him or that you seek out his company, either on or off the job. It does mean you assume his basic orientation is positive. Helping someone else through listening also requires that you accept without evaluation any comment or nonverbal signal from the other person.

Choose the Skills to Attain the Objectives

When you encounter someone who is emotional or who disagrees with you, you will be most effective as a listener if you act as if that person is the most important person in your world at the time. After your conversation is over, he won't be that important; but for that time, give him your undivided attention, both physical and mental. Realize the person is not thinking clearly and may not put the real cause of his problem into words at first, and possibly not at all.

An illustration of what happens in active listening is to imagine you have a glass that has in it two layers of liquids. The bottom layer is your favorite sipping beverage. For the sake of illustration, call that layer "Southern Comfort." Now imagine that some insensitive, unfeeling "Yankee" has carefully poured a layer of castor oil on top of the Southern Comfort. If you think of the Southern Comfort as the logical, capable person with whom you are accustomed to dealing, and the castor oil as a layer of emotion that has temporarily denied you access to the nectar, you can now see the job of active listening as tilting the glass very carefully so that the castor oil runs off and the Southern Comfort is left untainted. Any attempt to access the Southern Comfort with a straw will result in its contamination by the castor oil. After the castor oil is gone, you have the person whom you thought you hired in the first place, and your belief in his abilities will be justified.

Becoming an effective active listener means far more than just listening for information. Active listening depends upon the reflective statement, which was originally conceived by Carl Rogers as the primary instrument in his client-centered method of psychotherapy. In a reflective statement, you listen attentively to what the other person seems to be trying to convey and then provide him with a report. In that report you include three elements:

1. The facts as the other person has related them.
2. A word or two that describes how the other person seems to feel.
3. The use of the second person pronoun "you" to preface your description of the other person's feelings (optional). The advantage of using "you" is that it shows you recognize that the other person is under stress. On the other hand, some managers who are skilled listeners prefer to avoid the phrase "you feel." They think it sounds too much like psychotherapy.

Unless you specifically set aside the time and one or more other persons to help you practice, your chances of being able to assemble a reflective statement in the middle of a stressful conversation are probably slim. Suppose the other person has just made an emotion-laden comment, and you can't think of a thing to say. You have several options. One is to keep quiet and look directly into the other person's eyes. If it seems appropriate, add a sound, such as "oh" or "hmmm." Your objective is to show the other person you are concentrating on him to the exclusion of everything and everyone else. Another way to show concentration is by such nonverbal signals as setting aside something you were working on when he came in, closing your office door, pulling out the cord on your telephone, or moving away from your desk and sitting closer to him. Particularly in cases of disagreement, if the other person suddenly stops talking, you can prompt him with an "open-ended" question or a statement, both being intended as signals of your willingness to listen. Further, use such words as, "I'd be glad to hear more . . ." or "How does all this look to you?"

If the other person is loud, be loud with him. If your voice won't allow you to be loud, speak distinctly and more slowly than usual; face the client and lean toward him.

After the emotions or the disagreement are drained from the conversation, feel free to rephrase some of the facts the other party may have brought out, even though he hasn't asked for your comment. You can say something like, "Let me be sure I understand. You said . . . " This approach can help clarify an issue, and it makes you a more disciplined listener, because it makes you pay close attention.

You can also project implications by saying something like, "The upshot of all this could be a real change in . . . " The advantage to you is that, again, you become more disciplined as a listener. If your projection is wrong, you can usually be sure the speaker will correct you. Either way, it helps the speaker see that you are concerned with the facts of his situation. It also helps you to see if the other person is now in his adult state.

Avoid the Risks Inherent in the Skills

When you are actively listening to someone, you may find it tempting to nod your head, as if in agreement, to encourage him to keep talking. Don't do it. Many people who have learned their way through active listening have also learned that nodding their heads will be interpreted and remembered by the person with the problem as agreement, when in fact the listener either had no opinion on the statements or actively disagreed.

Active listening can be abused by reflecting everything anyone says, whether there is an emotional attachment or not. Several years ago I was teaching a seminar on communication, and at the break, two women asked me if I remembered so-and-so, who was in an earlier group. I did, and they pointed out that so-and-so had seized upon active listening and was using it in a most unusual way. As they told it, if one of them would say something about how hot it was outside, so-and-so would respond with something like, "You feel it is a hot day." As they talked, I began to realize that the reflective statement had provided that man with a new tool for casual conversation. Although he found it to be useful, it actually discouraged his associates from speaking with him. The lesson? Use reflective statements when the other person disagrees with you or is emotional. Don't use it in pastimes.

Active listening is a route to power. Become good at it and you will achieve, suprisingly, a measure of control over the actions of the persons to whom you listen that will sometimes frighten you. Persons to whom you have listened in critical situations will place extreme value upon any comment you make, even if they already know you are not technically qualified in a particular field. You might say, "Respect begets respect."

For that reason, do not make casual, quick replies to what seems like a routine question from someone to whom you have listened. He may act on your casual advice, and not always with the desired results.

Persons to whom you have listened and who have responded with a revelation of personal details or privately held opinions may later worry if they have said too much. Any indication on your part of not being careful of what you say can virtually eliminate any future exchanges of confidences between you.

Restating facts and speculating on implications are ideal follow-up techniques after the tense part of active listening is over. Used too early, however, either or both can result in your hearing what you may think are facts but are actually garbled information because of feelings that have not yet been drained.

The Rewards

Although active listening was originally conceived as a system of psychotherapy, its benefits to the technical manager will usually exceed its benefits to the person who is in the role of the client. True, the other person has been helped through a problem by your being the listener. As a rule, that person will be a much more effective performer after than before the listening took place. In fact, others will be challenged by your presence to be better at what they do. They know you believe in them. The Pygmalion effect may be in operation. The person with the problem now has some confirmation that he is important in your eyes, because of the time and care you took to hear him out. Don't be surprised if a person to whom you listen comes by later, maybe weeks later, and thanks you for the help you gave him. You made no suggestions; you gave no direction, but you helped, nevertheless.

You will also benefit from active listening by developing a better memory for facts. Some of the other benefits, however, are less obvious. For instance, you concentrate so completely when you are actively listening to the problems of another person (and setting aside your own problems) that you become more objective about your own problems.

The more you practice active listening, the easier it will be to remain in your adult ego state when you practice the techniques of assertion (Chapter 3). More specifically, if your instinctive reaction to pressure caused by someone else's communication is to fight or become aggressive, learning to be a good active listener will have a special benefit to you. Developing your listening abilities will allow you to avoid being caught up in your own emotions and sliding down the "fight" side of the mountain. That benefit will be useful in any situation, even those that do not require you to be an active listener.

One more reward: Listening without judging encourages truth. Your turning over control of the discussion to the other person and refraining from evaluating anything he says will lead him to believe that you can be trusted. As a result, he is more likely to reveal truth as he knows it than if you had tried to coax or threaten him to obtain the truth.

Fit the Skills to Yourself and Your Job

You may be in an environment where associates tend to raise their voices when they are under pressure. If someone raises his voice while he is speaking to you and expressing his emotions or his disagreement with your position, try to match the volume, pitch, and speed of his voice. This is not to make fun to him or to imitate him. On the contrary, it is a way for you to send a subtle signal that you recognize from the characteristics of his voice that the subject is extremely important to him. Think of yourself as an instructor in a special driver training car. You have a brake, but if you put your foot on it you will be moving away from being a listener and toward being a hands-on instructor. You have a steering wheel, but if you use it, you will be moving away from listening. You have an ejection button, too, and you can use it once (along with making an appointment to listen better later). Use it twice with the same person and the same problem, and the listening opportunity will be gone. In most cases, the volume and speed of his speech will subside, and you can allow yours to do the same.

Many managers are uncomfortable with using all three parts of the reflective statement described in the section "Choose the Skills to Attain the Objective." One alternative is attentive silence, possibly with an occasional monosyllable. Nonverbal signals, coupled with your silence, can transmit your interest and attention better than any words. Pull the cord out of your phone. Ask your secretary to hold all your calls—maybe even to rearrange your schedule for the next hour or so. Move away from behind your desk and sit near your visitor. Move your chair so you can't see the flow of traffic by your door.

There are at least two other alternatives. One is to reflect only the facts by restating them in the most neutral possible language. Another alternative is to reflect the facts and the apparently resulting emotions, but without using the word "you." Whichever alternative you like, or if you prefer the complete reflective statement, use as few words as you can. The fewer words you use, the more effective your listening will be in helping the other person solve his problem. Remember, his hands are on the steering wheel, not yours.

Becoming known as a good active listener will almost inevitably give you a time management problem. You will find that some people are so hungry for someone to listen to them that they will take every possible advantage of the time you have available. Given any chance at all, those people will take up more time than you can normally afford to spare. At that point you have several options, one of which is to recognize that active listening is somewhat like a capital investment in revenue-producing equipment, only with active listening, the investment is your time. It means a large investment up front, but offers a payoff in the reduced daily consumption of your time and more effective performance by the person to whom you have listened. Unlike a capital investment, however, the return on time invested in listening doesn't show up on any predictable schedule.

From time to time you will encounter associates on the job who have problems that are beyond their ability to solve or your time to listen enough to help them solve. Chapter 5 covers those situations where you have the problem and your emotions are involved. When someone is taking more of your time than you can possibly devote, the problem is yours, and the answer is in the *confrontation* aspect of self-disclosure.

A mild form of *confrontation* is simply to say that you do not have time at the moment (push the ejection button) and then make an appointment for a time when you can be a more effective listener. Having made such an appointment, keep it. Further, don't use that technique if your real objective is to avoid listening at all. Effective active listening is based upon your being receptive and the other person's being trusting. Delaying with the intention of avoiding the other person fits neither part of the specification.

Patience Gains Acceptance by Associates

The more you practice being the active listener, the easier it will be to apply the technique under challenging conditions, both public and private. As in the case of the assertive techniques, do not mention active listening, reflective statements, or any other technique discussed in this chapter. It is likely that you will, sooner or later, be accused by someone of having listened (not necessarily to that person) and then not having done anything about it. Let associates who criticize you in that manner learn by your performance. Let them learn that after you have listened actively to someone and "poured off the castor oil," you come to an understanding with the other party. For example, identify how many of the residual concerns are within your individual or joint control. If there are none, your job was purely that of the listener. If, on the other hand, you do have control or influence over the question at hand, join the other party in a problem-solving process. Whether you are listener or solver, report that back to that third party, then satisfy yourself that all parties interested in the discussion are aware of its resolution.

Problems for You to Solve

"I always pay close attention to what she says, but she says I don't listen to her."

My name is Tracy. I have been in supervision for almost ten years and have always received above-average performance ratings. One of the things I pride myself in is that I listen a lot more carefully to what my people are saying than most of the supervisors around here, including my boss. I almost always make notes on what my people say and I keep those notes for years. I also have a very good memory, so when it is not convenient to take notes, I listen even more carefully, and I usually remember all the important details.

Lots of times I have had people ask me who said what at the last meeting or even at a meeting that occurred over a year ago. I really get a kick out of being able to recall the details or produce a little notebook with the facts in it. Once in a while, I have had to rely on my notes to document someone's less than adequate performance.

It was a real shock last week when Donna told me during her performance review that I am not a good listener. I asked her what she meant, but all she would say was that being a tape recorder is not enough.

"I have heard a lot about how important it is to listen, but I just don't have the time."

I have been a supervising engineer for this outfit for over fifteen years. People call me by my nickname, Beck. If I would let them, they would also call upon my time almost anytime during the day. They always have something to talk about that has gone wrong and where and then they say they don't know what to do. And they talk and they talk and, if I would let them, they would talk my arm off.

I have a heavy load in my job, and there is no way I can spend all that time listening to them blather. I have learned to listen long enough to find out what they think is bothering them and then to tell them what I would do if the problem were mine.

Recently my boss went to a class on something she calls active listening. I don't know what all they talked about, but now she is criticizing me because I don't spend enough time listening to my people. As far as I can tell, that is exactly what it takes: Time. I don't see the payoff, but I do hear more of the criticism.

What I need is someone to tell me more about this listening bit than simply to take more time. I don't have the time, but I know I'd better get some help.

Cross-References within This Book

Chapter 10 enlarges upon the values of listening as a prelude to trying to secure an agreement or a workable compromise.

Problems Solved

"I always pay close attention to what she says, but she says I don't listen to her."

Tracy is justifiably proud of her ability to listen for and retain facts. Unfortunately, she doesn't realize that in taking notes and keeping them, she listens carefully, but not actively. Although her habit is suited for an unemotional, factual situation, it is unproductive when there is disagreement (even those that seem to be resolvable by facts) or the other person is being emotional. Donna was trying to tell Tracy to put down the notebook, get out of the role of tape recorder, and tune into the other person's feelings as well as her knowledge.

Tracy will have a hard time breaking the habits of ten years, particularly when people keep coming to her to have their memories refreshed. If her boss has enough sense to listen to Tracy's comments without trying to correct her, she will learn a lot by the boss's example. If the two of them will take a look at Chapters 7, 2, 4, and 6, in that order, of Kepner and Tregoe, *The New Rational Manager*, and Chapter 10 of this book they might find a way for Tracy to avoid further accusations of not listening. If they can enlist Donna without threatening her, Tracy's chances of learning what active listening is all about will be much higher.

"I have heard a lot about how important it is to listen, but I just don't have the time."

Beck sees listening as all expense and no return. As a supervising engineer, he has probably been exposed to present worth or internal rate of return calculations for proposed investments. He is a supervisor and a natural target for some of his people who want to complain. The fact that they keep coming back means he does spend time with them. He has yet, however, to develop the patience or the time management skills to avoid being overcome by the needs of his people to talk to him.

His respect for his people and their conversational needs is low, at best. He realizes he needs help, but the habits of fifteen years will be hard to break. He will benefit from an off-site training session in managing his listening. That training is more likely to help him if he has a chance to role play as the listener with a videotape replay. That training will be more effective if it can furnish data to convince Beck of the return on investment of his time. We can only hope Beck's boss can set an example of active listening based on her recent classroom experience.

References

Drakeford, John W. *The Awesome Power of the Listening Ear*. Word Books, Waco, Texas, 1967.

Fletcher, Joseph. *Situation Ethics: The New Morality*. Westminster Press, Philadelphia, 1966.

Gordon, Thomas. *Leader Effectiveness Training*. Bantam, New York, 1980.

Kepner, Charles H., and Benjamin B. Tregoe. *The New Rational Manager*. Kepner-Tregoe, Princeton, New Jersey, 1981.

Rogers, Carl R. *On Becoming a Person*. Houghton Mifflin, Boston, 1961.

Smith, Manuel J. *When I Say No, I Feel Guilty*. Bantam, New York, 1975.

5

Self-Disclosure Is Another Part of the Mountain

Having emotions or feelings is part of being a manager. You can manage your emotions by expressing them (self-disclosure). That way, they don't manage you, and they don't have to make conflict worse. In fact, talking about your reactions to something someone else has done is an ideal way to avoid criticizing someone destructively.

Self-disclosure includes critical confrontation, but it also includes complimentary confrontation. Both criticism and compliments, delivered in the right way, can help motivate someone in a direction acceptable to you. For instance, a properly delivered compliment of someone's performance will benefit not only that other person, but also you. Specifically, if you express your feelings clearly and honestly about what someone has done well, you can motivate him to more and better performance.

Appraise the Situation

Has something happened that is threatening to put your emotions in control of your speech and actions? If so, it's time to prepare for self-disclosure. It is easy to lose control because someone used the wrong tone of voice, made a careless eye movement, or did something that caused a problem. When the acts of another person arouse your emotion, and thereby your fighting instinct, do you usually react instantly? Do you blame, accuse, insinuate, bully, or imply? All of these reactions are aimed at the offender and are what Thomas Gordon calls "you messages." Some you messages are attempts to pass on the guilt for the failure to the other person. How many of these have you heard or said?

"You didn't give me enough time."

"Why didn't you . . . ?"

"I thought I could count on you."

Other you messages are attempts to act out the parent role and put the other person in the child role.

"Stop that."

"You should not . . ."

"You ought to . . ."

"That had better be the last time you . . ."

"If you don't stop that . . ."

Insinuations, labels, accusations, and implications also come from the parent persona.

"You sound like an engineer."

"Your judgment is usually better than that."

If your reaction is flight, your behavior is more subtle. You might hide anger, lie or cheat, vow to get even, change the subject, leave the room, start reading, gossip later, get sick, cry, or conform outwardly, often withholding vital technical or economic information.

Here is an example of how people will react to an unfavorable situation. It occurred a few years ago, when a group of women at a local engineering firm were carrying out an assignment to illustrate the wrong and right ways to use self-disclosure. The women gave us each a piece of paper and quickly showed us how to make a bird using the Japanese paper-folding art, origami. The teacher was easily able to produce a paper bird that when pulled in the right way would display a head and tail bobbing up and down. After the high-speed instructions, she told the rest of us to make a bird. I think two of the papers ended as gliders, and several were wadded up and used as basketballs with the nearest wastebasket as a hoop. When it was over, she asked what had happened. As you might guess, we blamed her. We pointed out that she had not given us enough time, she had not let us practice, and so on. The exercise made the women's point. We reacted emotionally and sought to blame them and their deficiencies as teachers for our failure.

Set the Objectives

The objectives of self-disclosure (often called confrontation) are to avoid fight and flight in situations where your emotions have been aroused by someone else's action or inaction. It includes situations in which those actions have pleased you, as well as the more obvious ones, in which you have been displeased. Self-disclosure requires you to be honest about how you feel and why. In other words, it requires you to "be real." It also requires you to translate that reality into clear speech, to describe your thoughts and emotions in sufficient detail for the other person to be aware of the consequences of what he said or did. Self-disclosure is the least used, most difficult, and most valuable skill for communication under stress.

Find the Effective Mental State

Prepare yourself to communicate from your adult, not your parent state, and say how you feel about what happened. More specifically, what you need to be effective in self-disclosure is a combination of clarity and congruence. Those words mean, first, being honest with yourself about why you reacted emotionally to another's act (you seldom react for the reason you think you did), and second, fitting your words to your feelings.

Perhaps in partial compensation for their advantage over women in being accepted as assertive, men have a terrible time learning how to be confrontative with self-disclosure. As boys we were told, "Men don't cry." Spartan youth were taught that feelings were a sign of weakness; they abhorred weakness, so they didn't allow themselves to express their feelings. The corporate environment usually reinforces the Spartan training. Firms generally accept a certain amount of assertive conversation on the part of its managers, but displays of temper or emotion are reserved for the top person and a few exceptions, whose other attributes counterbalance their outbursts of temper or joy. John Powell suggests another reason people avoid self-disclosure. He poses a question with the title of his book: *Why Am I Afraid to Tell You Who I Am?* His answer was, "If I do tell you who I am, you may not like me, and I am all I have."

Being a manager does not require that other people like you. It does require, however, that you report to them on the effects of their acts upon you, others, and the organization. It does not require that your report be consistent with the ways the other person communicates under stress. The opinions of the other person did guide the conversation while you were being the active listener, but those opinions are not trustworthy guides for you when you need self-disclosure.

The way a person's act affects you will vary with how you feel at the time and the significance of the act. But whatever the situation, the effective mental state for you in self-disclosure is the adult. It allows you to give a full and complete report of those effects as you see them.

Choose the Skills to Attain the Objectives

Here's a test. If the other person's acts have done no more than arouse your negative feelings, and if there are no significant effects on the department, your job, or any other part of the organization, forget the whole thing. If you spend all your time reacting to situations in which your negative emotions are aroused, you won't get much else done. When, however, those acts have not only caused your feelings to get into the act, but have had an effect on some aspect of your job, then it is time for self-disclosure. Furthermore, just as one of the times to use active listening is when the other person disagrees with something you have said, the time to use self-disclosure is when you disagree with another person. Restate the other person's position and the effects of that position upon your emotions and your job.

Think of self-disclosure as occurring in two stages. First, confront yourself, and then decide if and how to confront the other person. Contemplate the rewards of doing a good job at it. Assess the risk and overcome your reluctance to express your feelings. Second, report to the other person on what he did and its effects. The more quantitative you are in disclosing those effects, the more likely your report will be accepted and acted upon constructively. Don't spare any vital detail, no matter how difficult it is to talk about it. Make your words represent your feelings, and be yourself. Being yourself means matching what happened with how you feel about it and with what you say, not just what you think the organization expects you to say.

Do all you can to deliver a self-disclosure report so the other person thoroughly understands three things:

1. The act to which you refer.
2. How you feel about it, not how you think you should feel about it. (Sometimes you won't be able to find a word that accurately expresses how you feel. In such a case, describe the action you have thought about taking.)
3. The effects of that act upon your job, the project, the department, or the situation in general. Be as quantitative as your knowledge of the facts will permit.

Thomas Gordon calls this combination an "I message."

To illustrate a self-disclosure report, suppose someone in the group who failed at paper-folding knew better than to use you messages. Here's what he might have said: "I am totally frustrated. I didn't have enough instruction to do the job right, and I have spent about a half-hour without any useful results." Instead of saying he was frustrated, he might have said, "I feel like tearing up this piece of paper."

There is an aspect of trust involved in confrontation. Giving someone else a self-disclosure report means you are trusting him with knowledge of how you react to a certain kind of circumstance. In so doing, you trust that person not to resort to ridicule or otherwise use the knowledge to your disadvantage. The risk is inescapable, but the rewards are many.

Avoid the Risks Inherent with the Skills

A self-disclosure report involves risk and requires skill and determination on your part. On the other hand, it is infinitely superior to you messages in its effects on the downstream of the other person. To extend that superiority, do everything you can to avoid using "you" in an unpleasant situation or one that involves disagreement. Think of it as part of your job to condemn the sin and not the sinner.

After you have given your self-disclosure report, don't be surprised if the other person's nonverbal signals indicate he didn't get the word. Hardly anyone is accustomed to being given such a full and complete disclosure of the effects of his actions on someone else. If you think your report may not have registered, ask for some feedback using an *open-ended question* like this: "I know I don't always say just what I want to, but it is important to me that both of us have the same understanding of this situation. For that reason, I would appreciate your telling me what you think I was trying to say." Then shut up and wait.

If your best-transmitted report does not seem to be having the desired effect, you may be tempted to send the same message again. Don't. Such a report is a powerful tool but is not intended to punish. It is threatening enough as it is. Ask for feedback instead.

Until self-disclosure reports become a regular part of your communication spreadsheet, write them out before you give them. Let them sit overnight, or say them to an objective critic and ask him for feedback. If you can possibly find someone who has read Gordon's book and knows something about I messages, that person would make an ideal critic.

Another caution: Don't send self-disclosure reports unless you are skilled in active listening and are prepared to switch to it at the first evidence of an emotional reaction. The idea behind confrontation is to give the other person enough information for him to choose a more productive course of action. If his emotions take over, there is little reason to expect improvement. Most people learn as children how to respond to parents; they learn particularly well how to respond to punishment. A self-disclosure report, on the other hand, is not punishment and is not personal, if one adult is communicating with another about an act and its effects.

The caution list goes on. Don't include generalizations ?nd labels in a self-disclosure. Not only do labels think for you, they invariably convey meanings beyond what you intended. Instead, express your concerns about what a person may do and about the consequences.

The caution to avoid labels when thinking about other people is as important in positive situations as in negative ones. Phrase a compliment as a self-disclosure report, and make it specific. If you don't, you risk misinterpretation and awkward results. Several years ago, a symphony conductor complimented his drummer on having done a good job during the evening's rendition of Ravel's "Bolero." You might think both parties would come away benefited by the encounter. After all, the maestro gave a compliment, and the drummer was singled out for special praise. The lack of detail in the compliment, however, had an unfortunate result. The drummer decided the reason he received the compliment was that he played faster than normally. As a result, when the performance was repeated, the drummer played faster than ever. The maestro signaled to him to slow down, but the drummer assumed he should go even faster. The result was a disaster. Be specific when you give a compliment. Cite the action, report the effect on you, and report the effect on your job. When you compliment, unlike when you criticize, use the word "you" as many times as you wish.

Here's an old saying you can use as a guide: "Punish in private and praise in public." Be careful, however, the public praise doesn't translate to feelings of jealousy or favoritism by those whom you had no cause to compliment.

The payoff from confrontation may sound so good that you want to use it every time your emotions are aroused. Don't. If your job has not been affected and the only damage is to your ego, let it pass. Don't make every affront to your emotions a cause for a crusade. If you do, you will soon be treated like the shepherd boy who cried "Wolf!" every time he was frightened, whether the wolf was there or not. At first the other herders came to the rescue. One day they didn't; the wolf was real, and the boy paid the price. Problem messages are for situations where your emotions are only part of the action; the rest is job related.

The Rewards

Acquiring the skills of confrontation will help you develop the ability to manage difficult situations in which your feelings are active and might otherwise take control. Another advantage is that confrontation lessens any tendency you may have toward flight from stressful interpersonal situations. Further, you will learn how to transmit information that is valuable, even though unpopular, without making things worse. The highly specific " 'at-a-boys" you give to people when they have performed well will encourage more good performance. You will become practiced in identifying the real or root cause of your emotions and in deciding logically and unemotionally whether self-disclosure is appropriate. You will learn to be fully honest about your position in a critical but unemotional manner and not worry whether someone likes you afterward.

The rewards also include leaving without fear of conflict or of the consequences of self-disclosure of something negative. It means you carry no grudge. It means you and the other person can achieve a productive relationship, if not a close, personal one.

You have probably heard many times that there is nothing like a good fight. A true statement, if you place the emphasis on the word "good." A fight on its own merits will invariably degenerate into labeling and use of the word "you" in association with blaming, accusing, and implying. A "good" fight, in which all parties disclose themselves in I messages, can cleanse the atmosphere in a way no amount of active listening can ever do. Confrontation will not eliminate all personal dislikes, nor will it solve all disagreements. Its reward lies in the isolation of personal animosities and conflicts so they may be recognized and managed, rather than allowed to become the managers of the people who harbor them.

Perhaps the greatest value from becoming skilled at confrontation is discovering that the things most personal to you are shared by many. You find that the things about yourself that have bothered you or that you have felt should be kept hidden at all costs are things that concern practically everyone.

A positive self-disclosure is useful in giving compliments and unequaled in its value in timely motivation. Emery Air Freight picked it up a few years ago under the aegis of positive reinforcement and saved much more money in their containerization practices than by conventional tactics. Emery emphasized the need to reinforce as soon as the facts were in; to complement the words with appropriate nonverbals; to make the supervisor visit the work area of the subordinate to check the record and deliver the compliment; to reinforce any improvement at first, and to reinforce at random when the subordinate reached the desired performance level. In cases like Emery's, the word "you" is invaluable.

Fit the Skills to Yourself and Your Job

To many people, the word "confrontation" has a negative implication. If you see it that way, and if it means you cannot use it in a positive sense, think of it as "compliment." If the word "confrontation" is too strong even in negative situations, use the term "problem message." If that is still too strong, use "personal report" or "give a readout" or "I need to find a solution." The important thing is not to let the words get in the way of an extremely useful skill.

There will be times when, for one reason or another, you will choose not to confront. In fact, if your objective is for the other person to change his behavior, you do have some alternatives. For one, you could ignore the act entirely. The theory behind this approach is that, if the other person receives no strokes, either positive or negative, for what he is doing, he is less likely to keep doing it. The problem with ignoring is that he may be getting strokes from someone else for the same thing, and your attempts at changing performance by ignoring the act are worthless. You can increase the chances of success of ignoring the undesirable act by spending more time with the person and waiting for him to bring up the behavior you find objectionable.

Faced with continued unsatisfactory performance on the part of someone else, ask yourself if you are certain the other person knows what to expect. Use an open-ended question to learn what the other person thinks you want from him. The concentrate on the behavior and how you want it changed. You may find that the other person cannot correct the problem under any circumstances. The answer here lies in setting objectives and in training, not in confrontation.

Every now and then you will find that the other person simply does not agree with you about the significance of what he did. Not everyone has learned the same philosophies about what is ethical and right. Each person has a different value system. You may, over time, be able to redirect the performance of someone whose value system is different from yours. Your chances of such success are much greater if you use compliments coupled with active listening, rather than confrontation.

If you have ever been told you have a tendency toward sarcasm, or if you have a tendency to avoid confrontation at any cost, then use it when you least want to. Even if all you do is write self-disclosure reports from time to time and never deliver them, your skills will grow until you feel confident in putting your thoughts into speech.

Sometimes you may be part of the problem. If so, sit down with the other person, find a large piece of paper, and draw a line down the middle. Have a good eraser, because you will probably have to make several changes. On your side, state his position as well as you can. Ask him to state your position on his side of the paper. Include acts, organizational consequences, and effects on emotions. Be prepared to use active listening whenever you notice the other person's emotions coming forward. When each of you has listed the other person's point of view to his satisfaction, you are ready to seek a solution. It may be a compromise at first. The idea, however, is for both parties to walk away from the meeting free of restricting emotions. Do that a few times and eventually the two of you will turn from compromise to collaboration.

Use Patience to Gain Acceptance by Associates

The first time you confront with a self-disclosure report, be prepared for shocked surprise on the part of the other person. Also be prepared for his losing a good part of your message. Use an open-ended question to prompt feedback, then shut up and wait. If the other person's emotions are still in charge of his behavior, switch to active listening. In any event, do not give up. This will be a critical time in your managerial career and one that you will repeat many times. Give up now, and the repeat performances will become more difficult. See this one through, and they will become easier.

Confronting other people directly but without attacking is not likely to fit the corporate mold. You will be creating a new mold in which problem messages replace combat and evasion (flight). Those changes won't happen overnight; some of your associates will not change. For you, however, skill in self-disclosure will lead to self-control, and from there an ability to affect the actions of others. That skill will also lead to your being known for telling the truth.

Problems for You to Solve

"Why should I tell them how well they're doing? That's why they get paid."

My name is Drake. I have been a supervising engineering in this firm for almost three years. I do my job well and I expect the people who work for me to do the same. When they don't, I let them know in a hurry what they did wrong.

When they do things right, I feel like that is a compliment to the way I run things. They are paid to do a job, and so am I. I don't believe in babying anybody.

You would think I wouldn't have any real problems, but I do. About six months ago I got a new boss. He's been on my tail about what he sees as substandard productivity on my phases of three projects. He says the problem is that I don't handle my people right and I need to be more positive with them. When I asked what that meant, he said I shouldn't think that salaries and fringe benefits were sufficient rewards. I still don't know what that man is talking about. Do you?

"People know when they screw up."

People call me all sorts of things, but mainly by my nickname, Red. I have been a supervisor for over ten years. Almost all the people who report to me have been around for at least five years. They know their jobs, they know when they are out of line, and they know what I think about it. I don't go through any fancy personnel procedures. I give them a long, hard look, and they get the message.

Most of my people try to do things the way I want them done and don't give me any trouble. I'll admit there are a few who just seem to be coasting, but you have that kind in any outfit. I talk to the other supervisors about this every now and then. They all seem to have the same problems.

Everything would be okay except that this whole place is on a productivity kick, and I have already screwed everything down as tight as it'll go. I don't know what more I can do. What do you suggest?

"It's my duty to be sure they know what will happen."

My name is Spackler. I am an electrical engineer. I made supervisor about two weeks ago and I came into this job with some definite ideas about how to succeed at it. For example, when any of my guys cause me a problem, they hear about it right now. They know where they stand, and they know I don't pussyfoot around. I may even yell at them now and then and I sure as hell don't put up with a lot of excuses.

The main thing I try to accomplish when someone has goofed off is to be damned sure they know what will happen to them if they do it again. A couple of my guys have put me to the test, but they won't do it again. The way I see it, if you want to make it in management, everyone has to know that you mean business.

As I see it, my way of handling people has worked pretty well. In my last two performance reviews, however, my boss has talked about the creativity of the people in my section. It's nothing he has been able to put his finger on, but he has mentioned it twice. He says the technical output from my section has been accurate but run-of-the-mill.

I don't know what he expects. I make sure my guys put out a good job of engineering. I do that by emphasizing the use of approaches I know and trust.

"Want to succeed? Don't rock the boat."

My name is Rando. I have been in supervision for just over three years and I want to be promoted into management. I know the books and seminars all tell you that the way to get promoted is to do a good job and have someone picked out who can replace you. From what I can tell of this organization, there is more to it than that. For one thing, I am sure I don't want to make any enemies—at any level. I am also sure I don't want to make any mistakes.

I am extremely careful what I say to other managers and the people in my department. Even in situations where I think I'm getting the dirty end of the stick, I bite my tongue and try to find a solution that doesn't risk starting a conflict.

I guess any career has its share of problems, and mine is no exception. By that I mean that in a couple of instances I have been late and maybe a little indirect in keeping other managers informed about technical developments. There have been a couple of instances where I could have told another manager about a marketing aspect of a new product, but there were so many hard feelings about it that I decided to keep quiet. That manager really gave it to me when he finally got the word. I just let him rave.

One of my problems is with the drafters and technicians. Every now and then one of them will come pretty close to insubordination. I know that if I try to discipline one of them, there will be a big fuss, and that won't look good on my record.

Do you have any ideas I can try out? Remember, I don't want to get into anything controversial.

Problems Solved

"Why should I tell them how they're doing?"

Drake either doesn't see the value of compliments or just isn't comfortable with them. The way he looks at performance, you hire someone, he does the job, and you pay him. Until he realizes the psychological income is important to his associates, their performance will be that for which they are paid, but no more. If Drake's boss wants him to change, he can start by making sure they agree on what he expects in his performance. Next he can use positive self-disclosure on him, but only after he has shown some improvement.

"People know when they screw up."

Red lets his people know when their work has displeased him by a simple nonverbal signal. The problem is that they have little or no specifics. They don't know what he wants. If he would give them specific problem reports, their performance would improve. If he would give them positive disclosures, their productivity would "go out the roof."

"It's my duty to be sure."

Spakler doesn't know the difference between fighting and constructive confronting. His critical parent ego state blocks the creativity of his people. If Spakler is to meet the boss's expectations, it will be by converting his critical remarks to self-disclosures and by using positive I messages when one of the group has performed exceptionally well. His boss will need to be patient, persistent, and positive to effect a change in Spakler.

"Want to succeed? Don't rock the boat."

Rando has decided that the rule for success in this organization is, "Don't make anyone mad at you." His attempts to avoid problems will continue to cause him to withhold information and evade his responsibilities for discipline. Eventually he will be seen as ineffective by his superiors. If anyone is to break that pattern, it is Rando. He will learn to confront by giving someone else an I Message carefully and in private. If the first one goes at all well, he is on his way. If it doesn't, we can hope that his boss will encourage him to keep trying.

References

Gordon, Thomas. *Leader Effectiveness Training*. Bantam, New York, 1980.
Powell, John. *Why Am I Afraid to Tell You Who I Am?* Argus Communications, Niles, Illinois, 1969.

6

The Truth Will Out—Nonverbally

Voltaire said, "God gave man words to allow him to conceal his real meaning." Most of the information others receive from you comes through nonverbal channels. They may hear what you say but wonder what your words really mean, because they also hear your accent, your tone of voice, the pitch of your voice, your speaking volume, and your enunciation. They are aware of your silences. They may not know precisely what those nonverbal signals mean, but they will instinctively derive meaning from them.

If in addition to hearing you, others can see you, they will trust more of what they see than what they hear. They will notice the extent of your eye contact with them and the movements of your eyes. They will see the movements and positions of your hands, feet, legs, torso, and head. They may not have heard any theories about what those movements indicate, but they will invariably distrust what you say if they think your words are not supported by your movements.

Most of the people with whom you communicate will trust their sense of touch more than their sight or hearing. A handshake style to which they are not accustomed or a slap on the back when it seems out of place can confuse the receiver's understanding of even the most carefully chosen words.

Nonverbal communication is the parts and sum of body and eye movements, facial expressions, tone of voice, silences, physical contact, distance, and other subtle signals. Because of the number of channels by which nonverbal signals travel, it is not surprising that at least two-thirds of what you learn from face-to-face conversation comes through nonverbal channels. If you use it to transmit emotions, nonverbal communication carries over 90 percent of your message. Although speech and writing are essential in communication, nonverbal communication remains the most basic form for exchanging information among human beings.

Appraise the Situation

Researchers have learned a lot about the means by which nonverbal signals travel, but the transmission of and reception of nonverbals remains largely instinctive. Ideally, your nonverbal signals complement your words, but if you are not aware of those signals, they may contradict your words. If the relationship between your words and nonverbal signals is complementary, those with whom you converse will remember your words longer than your nonverbal signals. If your words and nonverbal signals do not complement each other, the listener may not remember your nonverbals, but he will reject your words, without knowing why.

The importance human beings attach to nonverbal signals is universal and without regard to their culture. As with your words, however, the interpretations of nonverbal transmissions vary within a nation or among groups of nations that allegedly "speak the same language." Those fine points of culture mean that although nonverbal communication is virtually impossible to ignore, delicate points may be easy to miss.

Animal lovers rely totally upon nonverbal communication, as do those "lower" animals with whom they communicate. In fact, animals seem to derive more information from humans than humans do from animals.

Why do people put so much faith in body movements? Because those body movements arise from the things that distinguish humans as a species. Desmond Morris's *Body Watching* traces the probable origins of our physical signals. They come from our movements and postures during reproduction, nursing, eating, fighting, and hunting. They predate language, but they have been modified by our cultures. A few have arisen within a culture as signals that allow communication exclusively among members of that culture.

Like most people, you are probably tuned to watching others' eye movements. When you see someone's eyes darting from one person to another and avoiding contact for any length of time, do you assume that person feels uneasy or self-conscious? You may not be aware that not all avoidance of eye contact is a sign of an unsure speaker. A person who avoids eye contact until a conversation starts may mean that person feels dominant. Widening of the eyes indicates surprise—voluntary if genuine; mock if staged. Narrowing of the eyes, other than to avoid the effect of bright light, indicates distaste or disdain.

Eye movement can tell something about a person's thinking habits.

For example, if a person's eyes shift to the left when pondering the answer to a question, it indicates right-brain domination, or a creative mind. The reverse means the person relies more on the left side of the brain, indicating the person is more logical than creative.

Eyebrows signal a change of mood. A frown usually has its basis in aggression but also indicates caution. Fearless aggression doesn't involve a frown. Raising the eyebrows to form furrows in the forehead indicates a desire to leave without the freedom to do so. Lowered eyebrows are for protection in combat. Quickly raising and lowering the eyebrows is a sign of recognition. A slower eyebrow "shrug" means distaste.

Head movements are easy to misinterpret. Nodding is a universal equivalent to agreeing, if done at the right speed. If done quickly, it is for emphasis. Bowing the head can be part of a formal greeting, a sign of respect, or a sign of submission. A rapid toss of the head is a sign of informal greeting or even agreement. Shaking the head usually means disagreement. The shake may go only to one side. A rapid wobbling of the head from side to side may accompany either speech that is positive or negative, but it is seen as negative.

Turning the head slowly to focus on something else can mean either dominance or boredom. Turning the head slightly away from someone means rejection. Lowering the head and the eyes is a signal of retreat; lowering just the head means a physical attack is imminent. Tilting the head back with the eyes level is an assertion of authority or superiority. Touch the side of your jaw or your temple while you are speaking and your listener will either decide you do not believe what you are saying or at least are uncertain of the facts.

The mouth and lips may reveal more than the eyes. A laugh and exposed lower teeth contradict each other. A hand over the mouth during speech means the speaker is hiding information, perhaps to avoid hurting the listener.

The shoulders reveal personal history. Those to whom life has been stressful, physically or mentally, will show it in hunched shoulders and stooping. Too much time slumped in an easy chair has the same effect. Shoulder shrugs have several meanings, all of which are negative.

The side of your hand you show in a gesture will send a message. For example, if you display the back of your hand while counting on your fingers, the viewer will see you as threatening. The open palm, on the other hand, shows you hold no weapon and mean no harm.

Legs are a giveaway. Rarely does anyone school himself to control leg movements. Standing with legs apart indicates confidence and stability. Standing with legs together indicates formality or even subordination. Sitting with the legs crossed means the speaker wants some distance between himself and the listener if the near leg is crossed over the far leg. The reverse means a desire for familiarity. The need to express distinction from someone will also express itself in how you place your legs by adopting a crossing pattern different from that of the other person. The tighter the legs are crossed and the further up the legs the crossing, the more defensive a person feels.

How you stand relative to another person affects the potential for conflict between you. Stand directly in front of another person with whom there is actual or potential conflict, and you increase the potential. The closer you stand, the greater the potential. Stand far enough from him and you reduce the potential. You are staying outside his "bubble" of personal space.

Another way to reduce conflict potential by observing personal space is to stand off to one side and orient yourself so that the line of your shoulders is roughly parallel to that of the other person. That means to stand so the two of you are facing almost the same direction. Think of it as trying to position yourself so that you and the other person can think of each other as solving a problem or taking advantage of a mutual opportunity. You are staying outside his personal space, but you are physically closer to him. You are taking advantage of the roughly pear-shaped cross-sections of each of your bubbles. The distance from the body to the circumference of personal space is much less at the body's sides than at the front or back. Done to the extreme, however, the sideways approach may cause frustration. If you detect that the other person wants to look directly at you, you can still minimize the potential for conflict by facing him, but at a distance that does not infringe on his space.

Compression of personal bubbles can make people so uncomfortable that they stop talking. A few years ago I heard an engineer from the John Deere company give an example of what bubble compression can do. The engineer was waiting for an elevator when the chief executive of the company walked up and engaged the engineer in conversation. The engineer appreciated the opportunity, and everything was fine until the elevator arrived. It was already crowded. The engineer and the chief executive had room to step into the elevator but little more than that. Their conversation, which had contained nothing that could be called restricted, stopped immediately. Put people too close together and they restrict communication.

A full beard projects increased masculinity. A clean-shaven male has reduced his masculinity and thereby potential for conflict with others. He hopes other males he meets will also avoid conflict. A partial beard is primarily cosmetic and often intended to hide or remedy what the wearer thinks will send an undesirable signal. A mustache wearer has preserved his masculinity without introducing the threat of a beard.

Research by Mehrabian showed that people receive information about a speaker's feelings in a face-to-face conversation by three primary channels:

1. 55 percent from what is seen;
2. 38 percent from tone of voice;
3. 7 percent from spoken words.

Even when the speaker is intent on transmitting facts, the receiver will still derive only about 20 percent of the information from the words and numbers.

The low degree of importance attached to words is also shown by the use of some words as nonverbals. In his *Beyond Words*, Randall Harrison says that "nonfluencies" such as "you know," "okay," "uh," and "well" are symptoms of stress or deception. Repeated first words and repeated other words give the speaker a way to hold the floor but have relationships to stress or deception similar to that of nonfluencies.

The nonverbal aspects of some verbals can affect others' opinions of you. Your use of slang, jargon, and acronyms can either signal that you are "with it" or alienate your listener. Poor grammar, relative to that of the listener or reader, suggests carelessness or ignorance. Greatly superior grammar to that of your listener may generate either respect or a suspicion that you are nonverbally expressing superiority. In either case, the listener will record the impression you make, rather than the expression intended in your words. Using "-ize" to convert a noun to a verb or "-wise" to convert it to an adjective suggests a disregard for the language, ignorance, or a transparent attempt to secure acceptance. Poor enunciation, particularly of long words, can result in lost meaning. Improper pronunciation can do likewise.

Performance also says more than words. The degree to which a manager observes schedules for reports and time cards says more about the importance he attaches to the documents and to the readers than any of their contents. A manager's observations of schedules for breaks, arriving, and leaving are a better indicator of his morale than what he says during a performance review or salary discussion.

Office geometry indicates a manager's preferred ego state. If his desk or a table is placed so that he can sit behind it, there is little reason to expect communication from that manager's adult ego state: parent, and maybe adaptive child, but not adult. If you have no choice but to sit behind a desk or table but want to engage a visitor in a conversation with both of you in your adult ego states, come out from behind your desk. If you want to increase the time you spend communicating from your adult state, arrange the furniture so no barriers exist between you and visitors.

Is your office neat or messy? The more the desk or table is in disarray, the bigger the barrier between you and your visitors. Is the door to your office open, ajar, or closed most of the time? The more it is open, the more likely communication with visitors will be from your adult state. Do visitors have to pass through the secretary's space? If they do, all your words about, "My door is always open," will go unheeded. It also shows a lack of respect for the secretary's "space."

Set the Objectives

The potential effects of nonverbal signals upon your listeners are enormous. That does not mean, however, to devote yourself to becoming a thespian or an outstanding orator by putting rocks in your mouth and strengthening your voice by shouting at the sea in the manner of Demosthenes. It does mean that you cannot escape sending nonverbal signals. Two basic objectives regarding nonverbal communication, therefore, are open to engineering managers. One objective is to do everything in your power to communicate nonverbally, so as to help your words serve their purpose. That means use nonverbals to complement or supplement your words: for example, graphs, pictures, or drawings in a report. It also means deciding in advance if in a particular encounter you are seeking short-term achievement, such as a workable compromise (Chapter 3), or building long-term trust.

The second objective is to be constantly aware of the nonverbal transmissions of others with whom you work. It means realizing that seldom will anyone say precisely what he means. In fact, many of your associates are so uncertain of their ability to use the language that they recognize no alternatives to gestures and nonfluencies.

Some of your associates will be aware of nonverbal communication and will have practiced many of the techniques recommended in this chapter. They may have achieved a measure of control over their hand and eye movements. On the other hand, the further the source of the nonverbal signal is from the head, the more likely it is to accurately reflect feelings, no matter how much training the person has had. People can and do train themselves in eye, head, and hand movements but almost never in leg and foot movements.

Select the Effective Mental State, and Communicate from It

As a manager, you can usually be most effective in a business conversation if you alternate among your adult, your positive, natural-child, your little-professor, and your nurturing-parent ego states. That means staying away from your adaptive child and critical parent states. Even if you can't remember all the aspects of nonverbal communication, if you have developed your confidence in self-disclosure (Chapter 5), most of your nonverbals will harmonize with your words. That means communicating openly and candidly without any attempt to injure someone or to hide information from him.

Choose the Skills to Attain the Objectives

You can train yourself to master the levels and styles of eye contact, head movement, shoulder movement, and hand gestures. For instance, in a one-on-one conversation, try to maintain constant eye contact when you are listening. When you are speaking, look at the other person about two-thirds of the time. More than that the listener will interpret as an attempt to push him around. Too little eye contact with your listener will cause him to doubt your sincerity.

If you are standing or sitting in front of a group, as part of a presentation perhaps, plan and use hand and arm gestures. If you attempt to avoid gestures entirely, you will come across as stiff and awkward, and your audience will remember that, rather than your words. On the other hand, if your gesturing is constant, it will be distracting to your audience. In addition to planning and rehearsing your gestures, you can avoid extremes by having a few "rest" positions for your hands. An effective rest position for your hands meets several requirements.

1. It allows you to stop all hand motion.
2. It allows you to restart hand motion instantly or gradually, according to that which best complements your verbal message.
3. It ensures that when your hands are in a rest position they do not send a nonverbal message.
4. It allows your hand, arm, and shoulder muscles to relax.

Some rest positions don't meet these requirements. If you clasp your hands behind your back ("parade rest," in the military), you project a rigidly controlled image that will usually vary from your intentions. If you put one or both hands in your pants pockets, you will increase the time to respond to the flow of your words. Moreover, if you have keys or coins in your pocket, your fingers will invariably find them. Distraction of your audience will follow.

Put your hands in your hip pockets, and response time will lengthen even more. Put your hands on your hips, and your audience will see you as more interested in establishing dominance over them than in communicating constructively. Fold your arms across your chest and they will conclude that you have a closed mind on the subject. Put your fingertips together in the manner of a church steeple and you will be seen as trying to impress others with your superiority.

Letting your hands hang loosely at your sides is a good rest position, except for two problems. You may find that your gestures don't stop, because your hands aren't "doing anything." Even if you can control this position sufficiently to turn off your gestures, your shoulder muscles will tire.

You may think that leaves the speaker's lectern as the basis of the ideal rest position. It isn't. If you have any tendency toward being a "white-knuckled" speaker, you will be tempted to hold on to a lectern as if it were a life preserver. Even if you are skilled in public speaking, the lectern is a trap. Use it to hold your notes, if you must, but keep your hands and elbows off. If you can get rid of the lectern entirely, do it.

Is anything left? Yes. Three rest positions meet all the specifications. First, you can let your right arm hang loosely while bending the left at the elbow such that your hand is in front of your belt buckle (or equivalent). The second position is to reverse the first. The third is to bend both arms. All three positions allow you to gesture with one or both arms and then to make your hands "disappear" without causing muscular strain.

From the moment you are in front of a group, strive for eye contact with the group and don't stop until your time is over. Look at everyone there for a second or so and then start over. If an exchange develops between you and someone in the group, concentrate on him as if you two were alone. If you want to encourage someone else to speak, look at him. Even if you are speaking to a group so large that you cannot be sure you have eye contact, look in the direction of individuals. Each one will be sure you are looking at him.

There will always be at least one who seems determined not to look at you. Don't give up. If you detect the slightest movement by that person, look at him, no matter where you are in your agenda.

How about your legs and feet? Unless you are a trained and practiced speaker, you will feel some fatigue after you have been on your feet for as little as fifteen minutes. If you can move around the room, do it. If you are stuck behind a lectern or a speaker's table and can't move around, you need a rest position for your feet that allows you to shift your weight. As in the rest position for your hands, find one for your feet that doesn't send its own nonverbal message. Don't try to stand at attention or even with your feet together. Don't stand on one foot. Don't bend your knees. Instead, stand with your feet about shoulder width apart, one foot about half its length in front of the other, and your legs straight but not rigid. This position allows you to minimize fatigue by shifting your weight imperceptibly from front to back and from side to side.

Clothes also carry nonverbal messages. Before a group, wear something similar to the clothes favored by your audience. If you are one of a group of speakers, all of whom are contributing to a presentation, coordinate your dress ahead of time. If you are asking for approval to commit money or other resources, a dark suit, a white blouse or shirt, and a dark tie will help establish the impression that you are conservative and can be trusted.

If your objective is to convince an audience to accept your position, adopt a conservative but popular hair style.

Avoid the Risks Inherent in the Skills

You can become an actor and expert at playing a role. You can learn to control certain nonverbal signals to the degree that they will complement your words, even when those words don't express your true feelings. You can learn all the proper hand gestures, posture, eye movements, and head movements. You can dress perfectly. You can learn this process of role playing so well that you lose the ability to express the truth and to confront others with the issues that are most important to you. You can learn this process so well that you set yourself apart from associates whose trust and respect you have worked to win.

The Rewards

The Rewards to You as a Communicator

Achieve mastery over your nonverbal signals and you will increase the accuracy of your listeners' understanding of what you say and the length of their memories. You will reinforce their acceptance of your well-intended, sincere words. Neither you nor your associates will know quite why, but they will trust you in matters beyond your formal presentations.

The child and parent ego states are sources of communication most responsible for nonverbal transmissions. The natural child state runs on emotion, makes no attempt to control nonverbals, and will usually be believed, although the message may be unpopular. The parent state runs on automatic and may try to control nonverbals by careful, but often transparent, discipline over gestures, posture, and voice modulation. Having digested this chapter, however, you know the risks of trying to deceive someone with words even when they are coupled with cultivated nonverbals. Avoiding attempts to deceive will help others receive and remember your total message more accurately and more completely.

Make it your practice to choose words that describe not only your technical or economic thoughts but your personal feelings about a problem. The result will be nonverbals that will have a complementary effect on your message. Couple those personal expressions with videotraining in the use of nonverbals, and your chances of obtaining agreement or making a successful presentation will approach their maxima. Even if complete agreement does not result, you will achieve either a workable compromise (Chapter 3) or a more precise focus on the source of disagreement.

Match your speech with all the other signals people hear and see while you speak, and you will encounter more compliments and fewer criticisms of your presentations. Make it a habit to coordinate your feelings, speech, and nonverbals in one-on-one or small, informal group meetings and you will build trust. You will find it becoming unnecessary to make explanations after the fact. You will find fewer people challenging what you said, even though they may not have fully received your message.

The Rewards to You as a Receiver of Communication

Be aware of nonverbal signals and you will be able to tell in the first minute or so whether to believe or doubt what you hear. You will be able to detect intentionally (but not accidentally) incomplete or misleading communication. In those cases where the speaker's words and nonverbal signals are in harmony, you will remember his message longer and in greater detail. You will not be misled by or critical of someone else's lack of ability or awareness of nonverbal communication. Although you will seldom be able to put a name on someone else's feelings, you will be aware that an underlying emotion exists and that it is interfering with that person's transmission or acceptance of facts. You will be able to predict the probable degree of success of a candidate or co-worker when he communicates under stress. You will be more aware than ever that words are often used to deceive.

Fit the Skills to Yourself and Your Job

Every engineer in management can benefit from practicing with a video camera, videotape, and monitor. Enlist the service of at least one candid observer who will respond freely to your open-ended questions after he views a tape of your performance. That practice is likely to concentrate on formal presentations, but it is equally as valuable when used in role playing critical situations, such as performance reviews, negotiations, and conflict resolution. Practicing before a camera and having at least one critic can overcome bad habits. You have probably picked up nonverbal techniques over the years that may send signals of which you are unaware and that may contradict what you want to say. Just seeing and hearing yourself in a role-playing situation will be enough to correct some of your unproductive nonverbals. The responses from a critic will focus on the things that are less obvious to you or which you might see as unimportant.

Training yourself to establish and maintain eye contact with members of a group can be made easier if you have several cameras or a group of cooperative associates. Ask those associates to help you master eye contact by holding their hands up until each one is sure you have looked at him for at least three seconds.

If your boss is like most managers, he will be only instinctively aware of his own nonverbal signals but will welcome some nonverbals on your part while disliking others. His principal interests in nonverbal communication may relate to your making presentations to clients and to the next higher level or two of management. Observe and remember those likes and dislikes.

Patience Gains Acceptance by Associates

Be content with small advances so that at most you will be seen as subtly different. Don't mention nonverbal communication, even in joking, until it is a common topic of conversation in your circles. Better yet, wait until the training and development department announces a course in nonverbal communication or your boss starts talking about its value. Mastering nonverbal communication skills is not an opportunity to demonstrate superiority over those who are less informed, nor is it a means of securing unfair advantage over others with whom you want a long-term, productive relationship. Nonverbal communication is a means of encouraging subordinates to harmonize what they say, feel, and show.

A Problem Solved

I once was an usher for several months in a new church. We didn't yet have a sanctuary, so services were held in the fellowship hall. It was air-conditioned and very attractive, but the chairs were the steel, folding variety. We ushers were accustomed to having to find seats for those families who invariably arrived at or slightly after the start of service. Often we could not find enough seats together, and the tardies had to divide. They didn't like that. We didn't like the confusion, and neither did the pastor.

It took us several weeks to realize what was happening. The custodians arranged the chairs the night before and placed them to allow sufficient leg room, but left no room between the sides of the chairs. The worshipers who arrived early had their choice of seats. They also had the freedom to preserve their personal "space bubbles" by leaving a vacant chair between themselves and someone already seated. As a result, although we nearly always had enough chairs for the late arrivals, they were scattered throughout the hall. Not good for those families who wanted to sit together.

Almost by accident we tried placing the chairs so that the lateral distance between them was about the width of a man's fist. The results were ideal. Our members thought nothing of occupying a chair next to one that was already taken. Fewer "singles" confronted the late arrivals. The weekly crisis of late arrivals disappeared.

References

Birdwhistell, Raymond L. *Kinesics and Context: Essays on Body Motion Communication*. University of Pennsylvania Press, Philadelphia, 1970.

Buck, Ross. *The Communication of Emotion*. Guilford, New York, 1984

Cooper, Ken. *Nonverbal Communication for Business Success*. AMACOM, New York, 1979.

Glaser, Rollin. *Nonverbal Sensitivity Indicator*: Organization Design and Development, Inc. Bryn Mawr, Pennsylvania, 1983.

Harrison, Randall P. *Beyond Words*. Prentice-Hall, Englewoods Cliffs, New Jersey, 1974.

Mehrabian, Albert. *Silent Messages*. Wadsworth, Belmont, California, 1981.

Morris, Desmond. *Body Watching*. Crown, New York, 1985.

Sielski, Lester M. "Understanding Body Language," *Personnel and Guidance Journal*, January, 1979.

7

They Pay Us to Communicate Facts

This chapter examines some of the reasons you can remember only about a quarter of what you hear, even if you know that someone is going to ask you about it or give you an exam on it. You will also learn the differences between the intensive and extensive meanings of words. You will learn that your best weapon for combating an incomplete, erroneous exchange of facts is feedback from listeners to you and from you to your listeners. You will learn that there is more benefit in seeking the background and implications of what seem to be facts, than there is in relying on the facts themselves. Sidney Smith offers a warning: "Don't tell of facts. I never believe facts, except figures.' " Lastly, you will learn that the better you are at communication, the more you will realize it is never complete and never accurate. You could also realize that it never occurs the way you think it does.

Appraise the Situation

Let's talk first about the barriers that prevent you from receiving and remembering information. One of the most important barriers, and one that you as a manager can do something about, is formal organization. The organization chart is supposed to show who reports to whom and who communicates with whom. Its very formality, however, is a barrier. You learned from early childhood that there are some things parents, teachers, and other authority figures don't want to hear. As a result, you filter the content of your speech. Many managers filter what they say to those who report to them, sometimes on the basis of the sensitivity of the information, and other times on where those persons fit into the organizational chart. Managerial attempts at filtration are usually defeated by the informal organization and the communication grapevine associated with it.

You may have a superior who communicates in ways intended to assert his authority. With him, you may react more to the expression of authority and less to the content of what he says.

The organization's grapevine not only counteracts managerial filtration, it provides a standard of "truth." If someone is trying to convey something to you, and it does not agree with what you have heard through the grapevine, you almost automatically become a poor listener.

Those who are in an audience with you can have an effect on how well you receive information. If you feel the audience does not expect you to accept what is being said, your listening ability suffers accordingly. That audience can discourage you from asking questions, because you don't want to look stupid. If your reluctance to question extends to not wanting to offer feedback to the speaker, the results will be little reception of what has been said, and even less recollection.

Another barrier to receiving information is that the listener has no standard framework for assigning priorities to the points the speaker makes. In such situations, you may jump to conclusions before the speaker has fully made his point. You may take pride in listening for just the facts, or listening for the bottom line. In your eagerness for a speaker to get to the point, you may infer things from the facts he presents that are unwarranted and based on your emotions.

You can be distracted by physical discomfort (John Gould said, "A lecture is an occasion when you numb one end to benefit the other"). Distractions of sight, sound, smell, or touch can interfere with your receiving information. Trying to pretend that the distraction doesn't exist can make it even worse. Other communications you have received can, if you don't temporarily set them aside, create an overload of competing messages.

It is virtually impossible to avoid having preconceived notions about a speaker and his topic. The saying "Don't bother me with the facts; I have already made up my mind," is an almost perfect barrier to receiving new information. It is equally easy to assume that a subject is above your intelligence or below it. If you assume the material is of no value, you are almost certain to tune out.

Your stereotypes and prejudices about people are easy to apply to someone who is speaking to you. You may decide they could not possibly understand the material; they are not qualified to present it, or their approach is too academic to be of any practical value. If either the speaker or the content arouses any negative association or experience, tune-out is inevitable.

Even in situations not complicated by all these distractions and prejudices, we could be misled by the speaker's using a word without realizing it has more than one meaning. Inaccurate reception because of unshared meanings can be understood by a fact derived from the dictionary: The most common five hundred words in the English language have an average of about twenty-eight meanings. As an example, the word "round" has over a hundred meanings that are sufficiently distinct to earn each of them a place in an unabridged dictionary.

Perhaps the most significant barrier to listening to another talk is that you may think listening is a sign of weakness. Most people were taught when and how to speak or to be quiet. Few, however, have ever been taught how to listen. You may have come to see listening as something that is fit only for psychologists, women, and grandparents. (Children often define grandparents as "parents who will listen to you.")

Some of the Barriers to Transmitting Information

Just as in the case of receiving information, the organization, and your place in it, can create transmission filters. If the speaker reports to the listener in the formal organization, it is a fortunate company that has created an environment in which the speaker can be fully open without fear of retribution. In many organizations the speaker who reports to a listener with a personal aversion to the subject will be circumspect in selecting information to be transmitted. Most executives over the years earn a reputation of reacting to bad news in one way or another. It may be that they don't like to hear bad news on Monday morning, or just that they don't like to hear things with which they disagree. Either way, the speaker is careful, and the listener does not get the full information. All of these barriers reflect the organization and the way people react to it.

Most of the barriers to transmitting can be laid at the door of you, the speaker. You were disorganized. You didn't know how much you wanted to say or in what order you wanted to say it. You didn't provide a road map or a timetable so that the listener would know what was going to happen in the next few minutes. Other than a few hand gestures, you provided no visual aids. You spoke more slowly than usual in the mistaken belief that your listeners would pay closer attention and remember more of what you said. You did not provide a way to learn by doing. (A Chinese proverb fits: "What I hear, I forget. What I see, I remember. What I do, I understand.") You were unaware of nonverbal feedback that could have suggested your listener was not listening. Your nonverbal signals may have been so strong that they overpowered the information you were trying to transmit. You felt so strongly about the subject that your emotions were in control, and you did not use self-disclosure (Chapter 5) to discharge those emotions before trying to convey the facts. You relied too much on saying little but being a good listener, and you relied too little on your speaking ability and asserting your position. You made the usually erroneous assumption that what you had to say was all that was important.

Most of the barriers to transmitting information come from our language itself. We often fail to realize that every word has two kinds of meaning. One is the meaning that is listed in the dictionary: the intensive meaning. The other is the extensive, or associative meaning. Such a meaning is in the mind of the listener, not in the word itself. In *Through the Looking Glass*, by Lewis Carroll, Humpty Dumpty declared an impossible goal: "When I use a word, it means just what I choose it to mean—neither more nor less." Casual, incorrect pronunciation is more likely to cause the listener to wonder if you have really mastered the language than to concentrate on the content of your speech. Emphasis on minor parts of speech, such as prepositions, interfere with the meanings carried by the major parts, such as verbs and nouns. Your use of jargon, slang, and familiar acronyms, however well-intended, will primarily transmit your interest in being "one of the group," rather than your desire to relay the information itself. Any negative implication about the ability of the listener to comprehend the material, even if unintentional, will stop the flow of information.

Set the Objectives

The objective of factual communication is the approximately equal sharing among two or more persons of certain information, its background, and its implications for action. Henry Brooks Adams advocates the use of facts: "Nothing in education is so astonishing as the amount of ignorance accumulated in the form of inert facts." Factual communication can flourish after the emotional problems have been overcome through active listening, assertion, and/or self-disclosure. If you are the listener, your obligations are to pay close attention, ignore any distracting habits the speaker may have, give feedback (even uninvited), and fit the messages into one of the processes outlined by Kepner and Tregoe (Chapters 3 and 10). Experience will teach you that you can put information into either situation appraisal, problem analysis, decision analysis, or potential problem analysis.

When it is your turn to speak, your objectives are to organize a message, send it, carefully label what is fact and what is not, and obtain feedback from your listeners to learn how much of what you said they received and how much they did not.

Select the Effective Mental State

If your desire is to provide helpful direction to the listener, this puts you in the nurturing parent ego state, which requires your listener to respond from his obedient child state. If, on the other hand, your desire is to provide information without giving direction, that communication comes from your adult state. It may even be time for you to get into your positive natural child state. If the emotions have been rinsed out, and the facts have been transmitted and confirmed between you and the other person, then the two of you can enjoy the accomplishment.

Choose the Skills to Attain the Objectives

A motto: This particular conversation will never happen again, so derive all you can from it.

When It's Your Turn to Speak

Without trying to discredit the institution of staff meetings (Chapter 12), the fact remains that most key decisions are either initiated or confirmed in one-on-one situations. Some of those meetings are chance encounters in the hall, on the golf course, or in the cafeteria. Even if the encounter is by chance, take a few seconds to talk through the "headlines" of the topic. If possible, propose an objective for the conversation. Make that objective the first headline. If you and your fellow communicator agree on the headlines, the rest of the conversation will be more effective in defining areas of agreement and will not require patching up later.

Move next to very short sentences that do little more than enlarge upon the headlines. While you speak, use succinct hand gestures to reinforce what you say about specifics. Use broad, sweeping hand gestures to reinforce generalities. Turn your palms up to confirm lack of information or lack of understanding.

You are almost certain to be interrupted. When it happens, be the attentive listener as long as the conversation relates to its original objective. When you have the floor again, relate your words to the original objective or to one of the headlines.

When all the feelings have been talked about, or at least set aside, there is still the matter of making your expression match the listener's impression. These two quantities are never equal. Their differences, however, can be reduced to a harmless minimum with follow-up by the speaker or feedback from the listener. The most effective way to complete a communication is for each party to tell the speaker what he thinks the speaker was trying to say. In an ideal communication environment, the speaker does not have to ask for feedback; the listener supplies it unasked.

In practice, most engineering managers are either anxious to escape from an unpleasant conversation or so interested in going ahead with the project that they neither request nor welcome feedback. Perhaps in recognition of their tendency toward early termination of a discussion, some engineering managers have learned to write a confirming memorandum as soon as they get back to their desks. Although some interpersonal problems may be left for later solving, the chances for longevity of the understanding increase markedly with the distribution of the memo.

Chapter 9 describes how to use an open-ended question to invite feedback. It isn't easy. Engineers who have been told how to use openended questions and who have agreed that such questions are ideal for encouraging feedback will, in "real life," revert to loaded questions that suggest their own answers. Even those managers who do ask openenders often react to the listener's "wrong" answer by trying to correct him prematurely. When you invite feedback from someone to whom you have just delivered an important message, be prepared to wait until your listener is finished—not finished listening, but finished reacting. Don't try to predict what he will say; be prepared for anything.

When feedback has taken you and your listener to a common understanding, you have one more thing to do to increase the accuracy of that understanding. Promise what you will do and when to follow up on the agreement you and the other person have made. Follow-up puts you in control of what happens next. With that control, however, comes the accountability—the blame or credit—for the effects of the communication.

In follow-up, promise to call or visit the listener and name a place, a time, and a purpose. That purpose may be to "see how all this sounds after a few days to ripen." Assume that, in spite of the appearance of complete agreement at the time of the discussion, the listener may have been misled by some unintended nonverbal signal or may have been so interested in one part of the conversation that he is confused about another. Keep the appointment.

If your operation is converting to participative decisionmaking, keep exchanging feedback and information until you are sure the other person or the rest of the group has all the facts you do. Their having the facts will, however, not guarantee anything about how they react. Moreover, don't assume that they will trust you. Don't assume you don't have to communicate as much just because you and your audience see each other frequently.

If you are in an organization that prides itself on informing only those who "need to know," be prepared for frequent fence-mending. It is far better to tell everyone you think may be able to contribute to the success of the project than just those who have a formal need to know. If your broader distribution of information results in damaging leaks, the or-

ganization has security and communication problems that extend beyond your exceeding the need-to-know list.

The grapevine is fast, inaccurate, and unstoppable. Facts, speed, and
accuracy can overcome the grapevine; anything less will fertilize it. An
example of such a fertilizer is for a speaker to start with, "To be perfectly
honest . . . ," or, "Speaking off the record . . . ," or any of dozens of other
phrases that imply privileged communication. Not only do such phrases
stimulate the grapevine, but your listener will wonder how much of
what you already have said can be trusted.

When It's Your Turn to Listen

This is not the time for active listening; this is a time to exchange facts
and ideas. That means, forget about the "you feel" or any kind of spec-
ulative statement about the other person's emotional state.

If you have a time problem, say so at the start. Don't rely on the
speaker's perception of your nonverbals, such as frequently checking
your watch, sighing heavily, or looking away. In fact, this is a time to
make your nonverbals complement your attention to the speaker. Move
closer or lean forward when the speaker seems to attach more importance to a topic, whether you think it's important or not. Achieve as
close to 100 percent eye contact as you can manage. Don't have anything
in your hands to fidget with. Sit still. If you're standing, minimize your
movement.

This is also a time for you to be aware of the speaker's nonverbals. If
he changes such signals as volume, pitch, tempo, or physical position,
be alert for a change in direction, content, or significance of what he
says next.

If you want to take notes, and you are one of several listeners, go
ahead. If you want to take notes in a one-on-one situation, sit beside
the speaker and let him see what you write. If you have time, seek his
concurrence on each point as you write it. If the two of you disagree,
divide the writing surface into two columns and enter his points on one
side and invite him to enter what he understands to be your position
on the other. If he doesn't care to cooperate to that extent, then you fill
out the points for both parties. That technique is particularly useful in
the initial attempt to establish what will be a binding contract.

You can listen far faster than anybody can speak. Take advantage of
it. Use the extra time to analyze what he is saying and to project what
he may say next. But don't try to analyze the speaker as a person, and
don't argue mentally with him. Listen for what seem to be facts, but
remember, facts are mostly history, rather than news, and may be inaccurate.

Listen for ways to learn from what is presented as factual. Facts have their backgrounds in someone's speech and/or actions. Facts may imply unstated concerns. Facts may lead you to an idea, projections, probabilities, and new ways of regarding the speaker's ideas.

If the facts or their derivatives are particularly important to you, state them in your own words and ask for confirmation from the speaker. Don't expect to be invited. Don't add, subtract, or modify anything. Don't use the feedback you give to correct the speaker. Don't state the feedback so as to indicate that you agree or disagree; use it only to confirm that you received his message accurately.

When the speaker replies, wait until he stops; don't "step on his lines," as they say in the theater. Once he has agreed with the factual feedback, you can extend the discussion to the unstated implications of what he has said. You are now the speaker, and it is up to you to ask for feedback, especially after you have proposed a significant implication of the facts. If you think it is to your advantage to have further discussion about something the speaker has said, restate his words in the form of a question. Such questions can start as, "Why?" "How to?" or "What if?" (Kepner and Tregoe's "manageable concerns," Chapter 3.)

Ask questions only to help your own understanding, not to control the speaker. If you are interested in the speaker's speculation on the implications of what he has said, use an open-ended question.

Avoid the Risks Inherent in the Skills

You may think that a conversation is going very well and that you and the speaker are effectively exchanging information without personality and emotional complications. You may be, therefore, unprepared for the other person's reaction to this freedom from emotional barriers. That freedom may tap a vein of communication that the other person has kept hidden for some time. Verbal Niagara. If you also have been waiting for a chance to talk about the topic, the result can easily be two parallel monologues, rather than a dialogue.

A parallel monologue can also start if the other person listens primarily for cues and then starts to talk on the assumption that you are primarily there to listen to him. A parallel monologue does not have to go very far before one or both parties sees it as an invitation to roller derby. If the other person has never learned how to confront someone through self-disclosure and to avoid generating a conflict thereby, the invitation is even more emphatic. This is not a time for you to teach confrontation, but it is a time to switch to active listening, or any of those parts of assertion that can help you deflect attempts at manipulation.

The Rewards

Become a skillful exchanger of facts. You will accumulate more information of value and in forms that are less distorted than if you had to obtain that information by continued questioning or by reliance on being a pure active listener. As the trust level between yourself and others increases, you will spend less time verifying information that is important to your work.

Customize to Fit Yourself and Your Job

You may, unfortunately, encounter those in your organization who react to ideas as follows: "If I haven't already thought of it, I don't like it. If I like it, I've already thought of it." About the only thing you can do in the presence of that attitude is to be patient. Remember: This is not a time to persuade, only a time to exchange facts.

If you work in an information economy, that means the organization expects you to observe the rule of "need-to-know." As ineffective as such regime usually is, it means you have to be particularly careful of what information you pass on and to whom.

Although you may see a discussion as significant and important, if you hear nothing of consequence from the other person and are aware that he is staring at you, you are in the presence of someone who appears to be an attentive listener but who uses tune-out. While you may be tempted to get into roller derby with him, it's time to conclude the discussion.

Other listeners will play the game of "my turn." They will pounce on something you say—using it as a cue—and follow with a series of statements based on, "Yes, and . . . " or "Yeah, but . . . " Don't try to change their habits. Get what information you can. Seek confirmation through feedback, and excuse yourself.

You won't be able to avoid thinking ahead to the next time you appraise a speaker's performance, especially if the speaker reports to you. For now, however, concentrate on receiving and understanding information.

Patience Gains Acceptance by Associates

Express. Don't try to impress. Don't use your knowledge or your speaking ability to enhance your image in the minds of others.

Problems for You to Solve

Who's on First?

Nick Thomas has worked for this firm for about fifteen years. Seven years ago he was promoted to project manager. His performance has been mixed. His final reports on consulting projects are meticulous, but his reputation among his subordinates is another matter. They like his polite, pleasant manner, but they often find themselves in conflict with one another because of a habit Thomas has. When he makes an assignment, he seldom defines carefully what he expects, nor does he always designate exactly who is responsible for a task.

Nick does know what he wants, but only when he doesn't see it! For example, he will ask someone to prepare a section of a report or perhaps a supporting figure. When the assignment is completed according to directions and given to Nick for approval, he always has a different idea about how to do it. This cycle occurs at least three times on every assignment. Nick's staff "jokes," but without laughter, that if a person gave him six ways to do a piece of work, he would always ask for a seventh.

Nick has another habit. He will state in a staff meeting that something needs to be addressed but does not assign it to any one person. A few days later his staff members may discover they are duplicating each other's efforts.

The staff is finding the situation increasingly difficult to accept. Nick's criticism of their work when the work was done as accurately as the assignment was made is demoralizing. His failure to specify a delegation is exasperating, especially when the project schedule is short and most of the staff is overcommitted.

Deadline

Samantha was thirty-one when she went to work for a large engineering consulting firm as a coordinator between the engineers and the services departments. As coordinator, she offered information on how to get the job done, who could do it, and how much other work was in the system. In itself, the job capacity held no authority to determine priorities. Any influence Samantha had with the service departments resulted from her personal efforts to be an effective communicator with her co-workers, to understand their needs as individual workers, and to be respectful of them as persons. Samantha expected the same consideration from those she worked for, but one of her first big disillusionments came when she had been at her job about a year.

Richard Jones was an experienced engineer recently hired by the firm as a supervisor for a small group of engineers who worked in a specialized area. The service departments had been working under exceptionally heavy workloads for about three weeks when Richard approached Samantha on Tuesday afternoon with a large job he needed to have completed by Friday. Samantha and Richard discussed the job requirements and the level of work currently in the service departments. Samantha expressed some doubts about being able to meet Richard's deadline, but Richard remained determined: It had to be Friday.

The workload did not get lighter in the next few days. Samantha periodically checked with the service departments about the status of Richard's job. She also kept checking with Richard to see if his schedule was the same. He was unwavering.

The last communication between Samantha and Richard was Friday afternoon around two o'clock. Richard stated that he must have his job by that evening. Samantha said that every effort was being made to get it done and she thought it would be done, but it was going to be close.

A few minutes before five, Samantha got the call from the service department that the job she needed for Richard was done. Samantha went immediately to pick it up, briefly expressed her gratitude to her co-workers, and went straight to Richard's office. Richard was not there and did not answer his page.

Samantha knew the job was important, so she took it to the project manager to make arrangements for mailing. When she told him what job she had and asked if he would have his secretary make the shipping arrangements, he responded that there was no rush. They would take care of it the first of next week. The project manager didn't understand why Richard had given Samantha that deadline.

Richard had left the office early to go home for the weekend.

Cross-References within This Book

No matter how factual the discussion may be, nonverbals will be a large part of the transmission. They are discussed in Chapter 6. Chapter 8 contains guidelines useful in transmitting facts without attempting to persuade the other person to accept them. Chapter 10 is a discussion of the rational aspects of decisionmaking, a good part of which involves the exchange of facts.

Problems Solved

Who's on First?

Part of Nick's problem may be that he sees every assignment or delegation as a mini-confrontation. Each assignment requires him to look someone in the eye and ask him to do something. It's easier to be more general in describing the task and directing who is to do it—almost as easy as the reports Nick writes so well. If you happen to have a Nick Thomas working for you, your job may be as simple as suggesting that he consider delegating and specifying assignments as examples of communicating facts, not interpersonal confrontations. The conversion of Thomas's style in giving directions will not happen overnight. He really doesn't like to do it and may never like it. The change you want, however, is in what he does, not in what he likes or dislikes. It might help him change if you can start him talking about his dislike of making assignments and then do some active listening until he has talked it out.

Deadline

One of the facts Richard is paid to communicate is the deadline for work important enough to merit having a deadline. If someone like Richard reports to you, carefully prepare an I message that spells out the consequences of what he did to Samantha's schedule, deliver it (orally) to him, and ask for feedback until you are certain he understands and agrees. He will have to mend his own fences with Samantha. Your job is to make sure he treats facts and associates with the respect they deserve.

There may be an underlying problem, too. Engineers in large, impersonal engineering firms often show little respect for female employees, particularly for those who do not have engineering degrees. Keep that in mind when you decide what to say to Richard and when you listen to his reply.

References

Adams, Henry Brooks, *in* Fitzhenry, Robert I. *Barnes and Noble Book of Quotations*. Barnes and Noble Books, New York, 1987, p. 112.

Hayakawa, S. I. *Language in Thought and Action*. Harcourt Brace Jovanovich, New York, 1972.

Kepner, Charles H., and Benjamin B. Tregoe. *The New Rational Manager*. Kepner-Tregoe, Princeton, New Jersey, 1981.

Reader's Digest. "Quotable Quotes," *Reader's Digest*, Vol. 60, No. 357, January, 1953, p. 50.

Smith, Sidney, *in* Fitzhenry, Robert I. *Barnes and Noble Book of Quotations*. Barnes and Noble Books, New York, 1987, p. 205.

8

Present and Inform; You Won't Need to Persuade

Let's start with some definitions. To *persuade* means to move another person to do something or to accept a belief. To *present*, on the other hand, means to submit for that other person's consideration. It offers the other person a chance to change his store of knowledge, but it does not attempt to cause him to change what he says or does.

To *inform* has many meanings. For the sake of our discussion, let's use this one: "to give someone information previously unknown to him." This chapter will help you develop the art of informing others by making thorough, even-handed presentations.

This chapter assumes that whenever you make a presentation, more will be at stake than the transfer of information purely for its own sake. It assumes you have a preference among the several courses of action available to the other person or to the group to whom you speak. It assumes that in the majority of organizational decisions you will be able to find more than one course of action that is acceptable to you. This chapter also offers several forms of visual aids and their applications.

Appraise the Situation

Sufficient preparation for making a formal presentation to a group can give you control over their stores of knowledge and, eventually, their decisions. Include in that preparation not only the words and the audiovisual, but your nonverbals as well. Once you learn to manage your reactions and your communication in a high-stress, give-and-take session, not only can you give effective presentations, you can manage them.

Even if the occasional is informal, your words and especially your nonverbal signals will have more effect on your career than they do in any other on-the-job opportunity for communication. In fact, your non-verbal skills will largely control the kind and amount of information the audience will accept and use in their decisions.

Formal presentations take on a life of their own. The formality starts with the first round of phone calls to see who can make which schedule and grows until the final roster and agenda are issued. However well intended were the original reasons for the presentation, by this time they will have become subordinate to other factors, including sensitive interpersonal relationships, conflicts over rank, and communication that favors impression over expression.

With such handicaps, the accurate, unbiased transmission and reception of information are nearly impossible. It's no wonder many formal presentations are privately regarded as empty recitals of what everyone already knows. No decisions will be made. No problems will be solved. Such presentations are better seen as a highly structured form of pas-times rather than as the activities they are intended to be. The communication is important more for its form than for its content.

Informal presentations have a head start, but are deceptive. As an engineering manager who is asked to "give the group a few of your thoughts on this matter," you may think the meeting is casual and without significant consequence. On the contrary, once the pastimes portion of time structuring has passed, you and your associates are ready to move into activities. In spite of the risks and rewards of the process, highly significant decisions about what to do next are often made at the end of an informal presentation for which you're not prepared. Because of the significance of the results of information presentations, you will be judged by what you say, how well organized you appear to be, how sensitive you are to the dynamics of the group, and the attitudes you display toward the members of the audience.

You may express a critical verb in grammatical form that creates re-sentment. You may be so informal in your choice of words that your otherwise well-made point will have no effect. You may use a term or word that has a connotation contrary to your intent and that either escapes or alienates your listeners.

Sometimes a presentation to one person, whether formal or informal, can have a major effect on your career. If the hearer is your superior, he will have a standard ego state reserved for such instances. He will probably communicate with you primarily from his critical-parent state, with a little from the nurturing side. His initial communication to you will probably include at least one reminder of his authority. With all the bad effects of communication from the critical-parent state, you might wonder why he uses it. It will help you to remember that your boss may have never seen any other style of communication. This is a cue to you to communicate from your positive adaptive-child state, not to change the objective of your presentation, but to show deference to the hearer's authority.

Although you will be trying scrupulously to maintain impartiality as you contrast the effects of various courses of action, most of those present will be selective listeners. If they like a given alternative, they may claim to have already thought of it. Let them! If they haven't thought of it, it will have to imply highly favorable results to them for it to earn the consideration it deserves.

Set the Broad Objectives

The broad objective of the "present and inform" style is to develop the client's trust in you.

When you make a presentation, especially to one or more persons outside your unit, think of every member of that group as a client. A client is someone who can be of benefit to you or your organization. A client is not always someone who will pay you for what you do, but is someone who can speak of you to others and thereby affect your professional career.

No matter how contentious a client may be, make it one of your objectives to make a presentation to him that starts as being unbiased and remains that way, no matter how he may respond. It is your responsibility to be effective in any presentation and to communicate effectively with any client. That means meeting any challenge, not always with an immediate answer, but without losing your control.

Recognize that to your client, you are many things. You are your organization, especially to outsiders. You are a counselor—a source of ideas on what can be done about a problem and an advisor about the results of each course of action. You are a neutral sounding board for the client's ideas. You are a source of vital information. You can be trusted with the client's information and to be objective in your opinions. Finally, you are a professional in the art of presentation.

Set the Specific Objective: Inform the Client and Allow Him to Persuade Himself

State your specific objectives like this:

> Having seen and listened to my presentation, this client will choose among the alternatives I list. To encourage that choice, I will describe each alternative so as to generate or at least encourage action by the client. I will avoid generalities and abstractions. To increase the degree of my satisfaction with the decision, I will make sure my organization can survive no matter which alternative the client chooses.

If one or more alternatives contains an element of time, I will be sure the client understands the payoff or problem associated with a delay. On the other hand, I will not expect the client to announce a decision at the end of my presentation.

Select the Effective Mental State

Presentation, even-handed and without attempt to influence, requires that you communicate primarily from your adult ego state. Use your positive adaptive-child state to express appreciation for comments that show interest in what you say, whether favorable or not. Do not in any way "talk down," especially if your listener knows your technical or economic knowledge is superior to his own.

Choose the Skills to Attain the Objectives

P. J. Marshall, a consultant in Houston, Texas, has some advice for those who would make presentations; it is called the "rule of three tens." The rule says that your eventual success in a presentation rests primarily upon (1) the first ten steps you take in entering a room, (2) the ten inches from the top of your head to just below your chin, and (3) your first ten words.

Two of those three factors are nonverbal. For that reason, whenever you can, videotape your presentation. Such practice will be even more effective if you enlist at least one objective critic who has an interest in seeing you do a good job. If you can't find a critic, let the tape sit overnight and watch it again the next day.

Do your research. Who will be at the presentation? What are they likely to know about their own needs? Something is not completely satisfactory to them: What is it? What might they not know how to handle in their present situation? Whom in your organization does the client know. Will anyone make a decision at this meeting? Who will make the decision? What will satisfy all three ego states of the decision-maker? Who is likely to talk a lot but can only advise?

Have a Technical Checklist

Will the facts stand the light of day and the heat of discussion? Did you check your references in the original? Can you quote someone's experience with the concepts you present? Have you had personal experience with those concepts? Which of your words permit misunderstanding—are there hidden meanings? Do your words imply your regard for the listeners as important? Do they demonstrate your regard for the listeners as capable?

Do your words reflect accurately the content of your ideas? Do they reflect your conviction as to relative importance and weights? Did you use the passive voice because you were not sure what you wanted to say or because you thought it sounded more authoritative?

Have an Editorial Checklist

Are the critical words in phrases simple and obviously intended to inform? If they aren't, start over and think in single, significant words. If that kind of thought process strikes you as too cumbersome or time-consuming, try thinking in headlines. Construct headlines that include a verb, to convey a sense of doing something or being something.

Next, expand the headlines to short sentences that either make statements or ask questions. Whatever you do, don't let yourself think in terms of file headings. There is no action in them, and presentations are intended to inform others about alternative actions.

Now expand each headline into a short, declarative sentence or a short question. Phrase such questions so they will stimulate the audience to think about your topic. Keep your sentences short throughout the presentation, an average of no more than seventeen words.

If you have only one topic or alternative, state it and follow with its likely results. If you can offer more than one, start by stating each as an expanded headline.

Don't use "you" or any of its forms in situations where the other person may feel threatened by what you or someone has said. For example, say, "The effect of that rejection was negative," rather than "That rejection of your idea may have a negative effect on your position." Another example: "The tide of opinion seems to be running the other way," rather than, "The tide of opinions seems to be running against you."

On the other hand, use "you," "your," and "yours" frequently when you are complimenting someone or acknowledging that he had made a contribution.

Restrict the use of "I" to those times when you are confessing uncertainties or asking for help. If you want to claim credit for having done something of benefit to the client, say it so as to use inanimate objects as subjects of your sentences. As an example, "Increasing the concentration of iron cut the processing time in half." It will be obvious from the rest of your presentation that you and/or your associates decided to up the iron content.

Use the passive voice when you want to emphasize what was done more than who did it, when you want to conceal the identity of the doer, or when you have no idea who did it. Don't think the passive voice will endow your presentation with a judicially detached attitude toward the subject.

The following examples will illustrate the passive voice and variations on it: A sentence in the passive voice will contain a form of the verb "to be" coupled with a past participle of a transitive verb. Transitive verbs describe an action directed toward an object. Here's an example: "The catalyst was added to the wrong component." That sentence is in the passive voice for two reasons. First, it contains the word "was." Second, it couples the "was" with "added," the past participle of "to add," a transitive verb. The reader will realize that someone made a mistake but will not know for sure who made it, even if the speaker gives the name of the operator in another sentence. You might observe that the sentence could stay in the passive voice but still reveal the guilty party. It would read, "The catalyst was added to the wrong component by the operator." Saying it that way gives more information, but uses more words than does the active voice.

Another form of the passive voice uses the all-purpose verb "to get." The 1980 edition of *Webster's New Collegiate Dictionary* lists seven synonyms for it, all having to do with "obtain." In practice, however, we often substitute it for "to be." Using the same example: "The catalyst got added to the wrong component." The grammar isn't good, but the voice is passive.

In the active voice, to provide as much information but in fewer words, the sentence would read like this: "The operator added the catalyst to the wrong component." Blunt, even accusatory, but informative and brief. Another alternative to identifying the operator is to use an inanimate object as the subject of the sentence like this: "The catalyst joined the wrong component."

Still another way to avoid accusing individuals in potentially difficult situations is to use the name of the employing organization as the subject, as in: "The Jackson firm added the catalyst to the wrong component." As a practical matter, an entire firm did not participate, but the operator's anonymity and that of his accountable superior are temporarily preserved.

Thinking in headlines and expressing them as expanded, but still short, sentences says things in the fewest words and is effective in keeping the facts straight. Unfortunately, the practice leads to shoddy presentations that may be hard for the audience to follow. Consider two ways to remedy the problem: (1) Use connective words and phrases, and (2) repeat a word or a derivative of it from the preceding sentence. Some examples are given below.

Use a connective word or phrase to connect these two sentences: "Painters have tried many ways to make paint stick to galvanized steel gutters. They have washed the galvanized with vinegar." The phrase, "for example," is a connective. Its function is to act as a road sign to tell the audience what kind of information is coming next. Applying that phrase to connect the two sentences: "Painters have tried many ways to make paint stick to galvanized steel gutters. For example, they have washed the galvanized with vinegar."

Repeat a word or a form of it to make the connection: Repeating "ways" helps bridge the two thoughts: "Painters have tried many ways to make paint stick to galvanized steel gutters. One of those ways has been to wash the galvanized with vinegar."

Don't use either connectives or repeated words to change the basic meaning of a sentence or its immediate successor. Their function is to assist the audience in absorbing what you say, not to convey facts.

If you have time to prepare, as you normally would for a formal presentation, outline it and do a final, double-spaced, sentence draft with margin notes. Do it even though you have been cautioned not to "stand up there and read to them." In a sentence draft, every sentence starts a new line. Format the page so the sentences occupy the right two-thirds of the page. In the left third of the page, enter the headlines (with which you started) along side the first sentence of the material you developed from each headline.

If you are trying to develop more engineering work for your firm, think of every oral presentation as having the potential of being a publicity release or a technical paper. Both will bring your ideas into contact with more people than will most verbal presentations.

Review the parts of Chapter 7 that cover listening for facts and be prepared to use those skills during the discussion after your presentation. Invariably you will hear comments that support or challenge what you have just said. In either case, rephrase what the speaker said and ask him how your understanding sounds to him. Be prepared for him to change his position once he hears an objective rendition of it from you. No matter how awkwardly the member of the audience has expressed himself, and no matter how negative he sounds, assume that your objective restatement of his words will yield valuable information to you. The same condition holds for what seems at first to be highly complimentary or supportive. When restated and offered for the audience member to contemplate, the support may turn out to have a narrower scope.

On the other hand, don't limit yourself to the technical or economic facts when you make a presentation. Avoiding that limitation is particularly important when you are discussing the problems that might arise from a given course of action. Include the implications and possible unexpected results owing to human reactions. But don't suggest that anyone in the listening group may have an emotional reaction to anything you have offered. If the decision-maker in the group brings up the emotional factor, consider it a sign that you have been understood.

Have a Checklist for the Overall Organization of What You Say

Build these steps into your presentation: First, state the client's objectives as you understand them. Suggest a separation of those objectives into three categories. First comes the thing they say they can't do without. Include with each a means of measurement. Then cover the things they want pretty badly and give each of them a weight that you think reflects the desires of the audience. If someone in the audience disagrees, check with the rest to see how they feel about it. If it means a change in your presentation, make a large, visible note of it and build it into the action alternatives that follow. This is one of the advantages of presenting and informing without trying to persuade. Make sure your words and nonverbals give equal treatment to each alternative and the potential problems associated with it.

Have a Checklist for the Question and Answer Period

Will you be able to obtain feedback? If so, admit you are never sure that you say what you intend and confess that you would appreciate hearing what the audience thinks you were trying to say. Will your feedback be limited to what you can see and hear from the audience? If so, divide your presentation into short segments and restate the message at the end of each segment.

Someone in the audience may need to make a speech. The speech can overrun your allotted time and interfere with the audience's absorption of what you say. Be prepared to use acknowledging and broken record from Chapter 3 to bring the discussion back on track.

Meet inaccurate criticisms with a few seconds' thoughtful evaluation and then acknowledge the critic and what he said. When the critic is through, state the facts as you know them. Meet accurate criticism with a few seconds' evaluation; admit the accuracy, admit your embarrassment or however you feel about it, and then offer to seek a solution.

If the critic is talking about a topic you want to pursue, borrow from Kepner and Tregoe's situation appraisal in Chapter 7 of their book and, with the critic's consent, restate the criticism as a question you can help answer. Have a chalk board or equivalent to write such questions so the critic can be sure he made his point. Whatever you do, don't give fight or flight a thought: hear him out. There is often someone in the audience who would love nothing better than to have the presentation turn into a roller derby session. Don't participate, no matter how well-qualified you are.

Have a Concluding Checklist

Build part of your summary around what the client group has talked about. If the client has made a decision, thank him. If the client has only heard you out, thank him for his courtesy. If the decision-maker has made his choice, include in your summary a plan for who will do what by when. Make promises you know you can keep.

If silence greets the end of your summary, tolerate it attentively. The audience is thinking, and time passes much faster to them than it does to you. Decide in advance how long you will allow the silence to run before you start asking open-ended questions.

Most of What They Remember Will Be from Your Nonverbal Messages or What Those Messages Reinforced

If someone asks a difficult question or disagrees, move closer to him, but don't lean over him or stand in any way that might suggest you are trying to dominate him. And don't violate his bubble or personal space. Concentrate completely on him and restate what he said. Don't mention emotions. This is a time for the communication of facts, not for active listening.

Vary the pitch and volume of your voice to provide verbal punctuation and emphasis. Use silences to emphasize what you have just said. If you wish to increase the amount of material they remember, speak faster, not slower.

Practice your gestures before a mirror or in front of a video camera, and don't be afraid to use them. But don't gesture continuously; have a "rest" position that you can enter and leave without creating an unintended gesture. Refer to the hand positions described in Chapter 5, and select the rest position you prefer.

Your posture can support your words or it can completely distract the audience. Don't slouch and don't stand on one foot. Keep one foot a little ahead of the other and shift your weight from one to the other to minimize fatigue. Stand erect but with your head tilted slightly forward. Practice by standing with your back against a wall until that position is natural to you.

If you can arrange it, have someone keep the video camera on you through the presentation. You will learn more about your communication habits from looking at the real thing than in any amount of practice sessions.

If you are expected to stand behind a lectern, don't lean on it. Don't even touch it. If you can, move around the room and approach the client, being careful not to invade his bubble of personal space.

Conservative dress is the best rule, especially when the client will hear alternatives that call for him to spend money. In most cases, that means a dark blue or gray suit or the usual navy blue jacket and gray slacks, both with a white shirt. If you are one of a presentation team, agree in advance who will wear what so you don't all come in the same outfit.

When you are speaking to the entire audience, look each person in the eye for a second or two. When you are speaking to one person, look him in the eye about 60 percent of the time. When you are listening, look directly at the speaker until he is through. It the speaker doesn't always look at you, look in the direction of his eyes and be prepared for the next time he does look.

Look for these nonverbals in the audience:

Nonverbal Signal	Interpretation
Arms crossed	Cold or not ready to agree
Eyes averted	Not comfortable with the situation
Legs and torso turned away	Distinctly uncomfortable
Fingers tapping the table	Heard enough
Stroking his chin	Thinking, interested

Use Visual Aids Carefully

Nothing has the impact of three-dimensional models. Make them so you can pick up each model (or parts of them) and carry them around the room while you talk about one at a time. Don't say anything more than what is needed to make your points. Don't rhapsodize about one model more than others, no matter how much you like it. Don't show a model of any solution that you think would be wrong for the client or for your organization.

Invite comment, but don't pass the models around. As good as they are, models cost more than other visual aids and take longer to prepare. There is always the risk that someone in the audience will insist on holding the model. Others are sure to want to hold it, too, and someone might drop it.

Think of paper flip charts as storyboards that may combine a simple sketch with the fewest words that make your point. Don't try to make more than one point with each storyboard. Don't put over three hundred characters on each storyboard. Make the characters large enough to be seen from the back row with the lights on. That means go to the room where you will make the presentation and see what size letters will be sufficient.

If you want point-by-point concentration by your audience, have a blank sheet between each message sheet, or have smaller pieces of paper that allow you to cover everything except the line under discussion.

Use colors to distinguish and to emphasize. Alternatively, leave some space and use it to add color with markers. Check out the markers to be sure they are not the kind that squeak or go temporarily dry. If it will help your presentation to have several charts visible at the same time, use paper pads and masking tape. They allow you to tear off and tape up, selectively. If you want to be sure you remember something, pencil it in the margin.

Chart boards imply permanence, but they can't be rolled up. Large, vinyl and leather carrying cases help reduce the difficulties of transporting chart boards. They are made of foamed polystyrene, which means they are rigid and light enough to be easily handled during a presentation.

Stay away from slides unless you have ideal photographs, and there is no other way to present their message. Use two-projector slide shows only if you can't come up with a simpler visual aid.

Overhead transparencies, like slide shows, require you to turn the lights off. The client may become drowsy and will have a hard time taking notes he can read later. Stay away from overhead transparencies unless you have too little time to prepare a flip chart. Don't copy from anything that was intended to be read and then use it as a slide or a transparency. Unless it is very unusual, it will have too many keystrokes on it to be followed and understood by your audience.

Graphs and tables are ideal visual aids, but don't use them just to present data. Before you even start to sketch the outlines of a graph, write what you want it to convey. Count the number of keystrokes to be sure you are below three hundred. Give it a title that conveys the message. If the graph you prepare will substantiate the message only if you compress or elongate a scale, rethink the message.

Give tables titles that carry the message you have in mind. If any of the entries are the results of a calculation, include the details of one such entry.

See Chapter 5 of Terry Smith's *Making Successful Presentations* for a comparison of several ways of graphing data. If you use bar charts, choose vertical bars to represent quantities such as weight, cost, temperature, and height. Use horizontal bars to represent speed, time, width, and length. Don't hand out anything for the client to read until you are about to leave or are done talking.

Avoid the Risks Inherent with the Skills

Don't become so enamored with being factual that you underestimate the client's emotional needs. Thorough research too thoroughly observed will inhibit your expression of the chance and probability that are always present.

Your client is aware that you know more than he does about the subject. Emphasize that knowledge by communicating from your parent ego state to the child state of the client, and you create pressure on the client. Clients who are aware they are being pressured will react emotionally. They will become obstinate and do nothing or choose a course of action that is neither to their benefit or yours.

Form that is too well polished will dominate function. Too much attention to impressing someone of authority in the audience will sterilize what you say. You will be too nervous and uncomfortable to give a balanced presentation. The targeted person will miss the point and will form an incorrect, unflattering concept of your abilities. As an example, professional flip charts can emphasize form over function. The client will forget important details, and you will lose technical credibility. The emphasis on being objective about all of the alternatives may affect your judgment by inhibiting your "gut" feelings.

Some of your audience will be accustomed to technological presentations in which the speakers prefer chronology and a sequential logic. They may reject headlines, saying, "Headlines belong in newspapers, and this isn't a newspaper." Others may expect a slow build-up to a vigorous climax, and any other approach may suggest to them that you don't really believe what you say. Approach perfection in your preparation and you may find yourself resenting interruptions. Or there may be no interruptions; the audience is spellbound. If that happens, you will miss some valuable feedback.

The Rewards

Do your job well, and the adult, parent, and child ego states of the client will be satisfied. That satisfaction is essential to progress for your organization and to you personally. Become skilled in presentations, and you will set an example for others. You will be able to avoid emotional conflict while concentrating on the data, the logic, and the audience's reactions.

Customize to Fit Yourself and Your Job

If you know someone in the audience is better informed than you on part of the subject, it will make him feel more favorable to your proposition if he can contribute and you rephrase what he says. That doesn't mean for you to feign ignorance, it just means to acknowledge his professional knowledge.

You can't know it all. You don't have to answer every question, but you can promise to follow up. When you don't have the facts, admit it. But don't apologize, and don't make excuses. If you feel embarrassment, say so.

Don't try to be funny by telling what you think is a joke. If the audience finds humor in something you say or do, be prepared to join them, even if they are laughing at an error you made. Avoid racist or sexist terms and avoid anything religious or political.

Patience Gains Acceptance by Associates

The people you work with are probably accustomed to managers who, when they speak, communicate from their parent ego state and address the child state of a client. Moreover, many of your peers in management would not think of the other person as a client unless he were already a paying customer. Some of those peers will have developed the habit of communicating from their adaptive-child states to the nurturing-parent state of a paying customer or anyone who has authority or influence over them.

Expect most of your associates to be convinced that in a presentation they must persuade the audience to a given course of action. They believe that if you don't persuade, you haven't communicated. They emphasize the relative authority levels among the client group and their own. They have been trained to put on the pressure when the client wavers.

They do not welcome searching questions. They do not welcome intensive communication surrounding critical decisions. They pride themselves on their ability to survive and win a roller derby. That includes effective, even memorable, put-downs of obnoxious clients.

They will find it strange when you treat a difficult audience with respect. They will find it strange that you give the most even-handed presentation the data allow. They will not understand your motives in acting as a counselor to the client, nor will they understand how you can communicate from your adult even in the most stressful situations.

Problems for You to Solve

"I am always prepared, and my presentations are always well organized."

My name is Venze. I am a mechanical engineer. Making presentations to clients is part of my job. I do my job as well as anyone else around here. My strengths are (1) knowing everything I can about the people who will be in the audience, (2) knowing more than any of them do about the subject, (3) telling them exactly what I think they should do, and (4) establishing and maintaining control throughout a presentation. My old boss complimented me often on how well I ran a presentation and made sure no one went into oral Niagara. Recently a new boss took over our group. He has heard me give a couple of presentations but hasn't had much to say, other than that I am well prepared. This morning he told me that one of the other engineers in the group is going to give a particularly sensitive presentation to a bunch of visiting firemen. I was sure I would be picked for the job. This could be a bad omen for my career, and I'm not sure what to do. Can you suggest anything?

"My presentations are complete and perfect."

Robert is a marketing representative for a well-established engineering firm. He has worked for the firm for several years and is following in his father's footsteps. Robert gives the impression that he is confident and well-informed. In conversations involving only a few persons, Robert presents himself well.

Robert's firm has recently developed some powerful computer programs for the utility industry. Part of Robert's job is to market these programs. It is also his job to promote within the firm the capabilities of the new programs. As part of the marketing effort, Robert was asked to develop a presentation to inform his co-workers about these capabilities. Robert was very thorough in his preparation. The presentation in its final form ran about two and a half hours. It was filled with slides, clever demonstrations, and periods of lecturing.

For the week after the first presentation the grapevine was full of words like "overkill" and "boring." In addition, there were many comments about the way Robert delivered the lectures. He looks down (as though he were reading notes) when he speaks to an audience. He makes almost no eye contact.

You are Robert's boss; you know that the firm's clients will never sit through anything like what Robert delivered. The first presentation to a client group is scheduled as part of a national meeting in two weeks. You would not consider cancelling.

Problems Solved

"I am always prepared, and my presentations are always well organized."

Venze operates only out of his parent ego state. Putting it another way, he "sells down." His tone of voice carries the unspoken message,

"Everything I say is Important." He regards the members of his audiences as his technological inferiors, even as children whom he expects to be grateful and obey. He would probably never admit the importance of any of that, especially since his boss has complimented him on his control of presentations.

If there is one suggestion that may rescue him from this bind, it is to ask him to think of all the people who have sold him something. Then ask him to think of the ones (if any) whose style of selling was such that he came away liking what happened. Chances are that the ones he liked "sold up." They saw him as being in a superior role, if only because of his education. They didn't try to control him during the sale, but responded to what they saw his needs to be. They operated out of their positive adaptive child ego states and tried to communicate with his nurturing-parent state. A few even have conversed with him on an adult-to-adult basis.

"My presentations are complete and perfect."

The most obvious place to start is with Robert's lack of eye contact. He needs practice and a lot of it. Put him in front of some of some colleagues and ask him to look at first one then the other while he delivers the lecture part of the presentation. Ask him to look at each one for a second or two, but not to stare at anyone.

The next part is harder. Ask him to prepare a situation analysis (according to Chapter 10) as if he were a prospective client. Expect to spend some time helping him sort out the client's priorities for computer programs and how long he wants to sit still for a presentation. Then ask him to align each part of his presentation with its closes relative in those priorities. By this time, Robert should be able to abandon some of his cherished slides and other elements that were aimed at his priorities, rather than at those of the client.

You may have to limit Robert to a given number of minutes for the presentation and some more time for questions. Use the priorities you developed in the situation appraisal to set the time limits. The rest of the development of Robert as the presenter is practice and critique of such things as the volume and variation of pitch of his voice.

References

Coxe, Weld. *Marketing Architectural and Engineering Services.* 2d ed. Van Nostrand Reinhold, New York, 1983.

"The Engineering of Agreement." 2d ed., Roundtable Films, Beverly Hills, California, 1978.

Jones, G. *How to Market Professional Design Services*. 2d ed., McGraw-Hill, New York, 1983.

Kepner, Charles R., and Benjamin B. Tregoe. *The New Rational Manager*. Kepner-Tregoe, Princeton, New Jersey, 1981.

Smith, Terry C. *Making Successful Presentations*. Wiley, New York, 1984.

9

Listening and the Right Verbs Can Help You Persuade

Those whom you will persuade to change their actions will do so to your satisfaction only when they are convinced you recognize their personal importance and ability. Some attempts to persuade others to change what they do will fail. The results of most other attempts to persuade are marginal and short-lived. A guideline: He who is convinced against his will is of his own opinion still. When you are trying to persuade someone over whom you have little influence and no authority, your most effective technique is active listening. You can measure your persuasive skills by the accuracy and alacrity of the feedback you receive and by what the client does later.

You can choose among six moods and combinations of verbs when you try to persuade a subordinate to change his performance. Those verb combinations vary in the efficiency with which they convey meaning and in their likelihood of creating resistance.

Appraise the Situation

Persuasion Means Orders, to a Subordinate

Persuasion is one of the major purposes of conversation. The other purposes are exchanging information, discharging feelings, cementing relationships with small talk, and making ourselves look good to others. The practical expressions of persuasion can range from a direct order to the most subtle hint. No matter where your intent may fall on that spectrum, you are trying to communicate with a subordinate to make him change what he is doing. You may have power over him because of what is written in an organizational chart, and you may feel certain of what he will eventually do when you give him a direct order. You may have learned to expect some signals of resistance on his part while being confident that he will eventually obey. But he can fail to cooperate in an infinite number of ways, one of which is outright, obvious disobedience. Other ways are practically invisible and impossible for you to detect until a crisis results from his failure to comply. His little-professor ego state can also be maliciously obedient.

You may pride yourself for being the "boss who never gave an order." You may strive to be known as the boss who gives only the most gentle of suggestions or who is always polite when he asks you to do something. What you may not realize is that it takes more than your orders or suggestions before someone does your bidding, does it well, and does it on time. It also means that for your particular style of persuading to be effective requires precise control over your communication, particularly a careful choice of verbs.

You may think you understand a subordinate's technical position and that all you have to do is to demonstrate the superior logic of your position. Or you may think that the success of your attempt to persuade him rests solely on your knowing more about the subject than he does. What you may not realize is that any communication from you that he sees as an attempt to demonstrate your superiority will mean failure in your attempt to persuade.

You may think you understand how he feels about the subject, but that understanding can never be complete. Further, if you try to convince him that you understand how he feels, your attempt to persuade will fail.

Most of those whom you try to persuade will appear initially to differ with your position. Many of them will appear to differ with you on a personal basis. They may emphasize the differences just because you are the person who is trying to persuade them.

If You Don't Have the Power, Try Persuasion

The person to whom you make a presentation that is intended to persuade will not have spent nearly the amount of time preparing for the discussion that you have. That difference in preparation is likely to lead to several silent questions by that person. "What's in it for me?" or "What does he want this time?" The difference in preparation will also lead to objections that are poorly formed, irrelevant, or undeservedly critical.

As the target of your persuasive speech, the listener may see or hear things in your sounds or movements that direct his thinking to something else or leave him almost incapable of examining rationally what you have said. That kind of reaction to your nonverbal signals will recall the barriers to listening cited in Chapter 7. The art of persuasion includes your being ready for any kind of reaction from the client with any degree of intensity. This use of the word "client" is intended to encourage you to think of a person of whom you expect change, who may even report to you, and as someone who reserves a degree of choice and deserves your respect.

Set the Objectives

The primary objective of persuasion is a lasting, positive influence on the client's performance. A secondary objective is to create in the client's mind an image of you as a professional who can be a source of guidance and help. In those instances in which the client reports to you in the formal organization, persuasion has the objective of creating trust of your motives in the client's mind. That element of trust means that you are accepted, but not necessarily acclaimed.

Select the Effective Mental State

If you want acceptance instead of resistance, communicate from your adult ego state. Be logical and factual, and address the client's adult state as long as he is receptive to logic and facts. Address the client's child state if you receive an emotion-laden response. Address the parent state if you receive a response that is intended as critical of your position. Whatever the provocation or whatever your preferred practice as manager, don't allow yourself to communicate from your critical-parent or negative adaptive-child state.

Sometimes you can persuade by communicating from your positive adaptive-child state and addressing the client's nurturing-parent state. That path can cause problems of its own. The client's reaction can be, "You were great at opening the discussion, but I don't think you're up to the details."

Choose the Skills to Attain the Objectives

When you have no authority over the client, make your pitch and be prepared for silence and/or disagreement. (Before you go any further, rehearse the techniques of open-ended questions and reflective statements in Chapter 4. Then use the time you have left to prepare to present your ideas according to Chapter 7.)

When you have finished the presentation, or at least have come to a stopping point, you may encounter anything from silence to a reaction characterized by its volume, if not its logic. If there is only silence, this is where your practice with open-ended questions can pay off. You don't actually have to ask a question. You can say something like "I'd like very much to hear how you react to those ideas."

Both the silence and the reactions can mean complete agreement. Loud applause can be interrupted to mean personal acclaim for the speaker. It seldom does.

Persuasion means change for the client—a change he didn't plan or design. If this is the first he has heard of it, disagreement is inevitable. Pose your open question or statement so that it is not a subtle attempt to encourage agreement, and you will reach the client's true concerns much quicker. If you want more than a superficial, temporary change, now is the time to show the client by what you say and how you say it that you recognize his personal importance and his personal capabilities.

A well-delivered open question—and it may take more than one—will evoke a response that targets one or more of the client's concerns. Those concerns may appear to you to be only obliquely related to your propositions. You may think it's time to point out that the purpose of the discussion is different from his concern. Don't; he's still thinking things through.

You are now at the first critical point of your presentation. Most managers who have come from a technological background will instinctively try to refute or discredit the objection or the objector. Such managers act the part of the critical parent to the objector's child. The earlier in the discussion you do that, the sooner you have lost all chance of success. Instead of trying to counter objections, think out loud about what he said, but don't pass judgment on it. Put what he said in your own words and run them back by the objector while saying that you want to check your understanding of the objection. A large supply of unemotional patience is essential. It may even help to comment to the objector that you think there must be some reason for the objection. If the objector makes a valid point, recognize it. After you have encouraged the client to explore his objection thoroughly, you may want to ask him for suggestions on how to minimize the problem.

The client may respond to your open question with what sounds like an accusation. If your reaction is to straighten him out or to abandon ship, you can be excused; both are normal to our species. But you didn't come here to do what is normal, you came to persuade. So switch immediately to acknowledging, negative assertion, or negative inquiry, according to the needs of the situation. They are illustrated in Chapter 3.

When all the objections have been rinsed out, it is time to be alert for any question or indication that the client has some interest in the proposal. This is the point at which the experienced salesperson asks, "How shall we ship it?" You may not see yourself as an experienced salesperson, only as an engineer who is trying to be a manager. You can ask any question or make any statement that invites the client to expand on his interest. You are almost home, but the critical junctures aren't over.

Now come some questions about the best way to implement the change. Don't fall into the trap of being so happy that you have achieved a measure of agreement that you climb into your positive natural-child state and give away the store. Now it is time for very careful negotiation, point by point, in which you yield only on those points that will not injure your original objective. One more step. Be sure you and the client examine the possible adverse consequences of each course of action you examine. Then think about how to implement actions so as to minimize the effects of those consequences.

You have persuaded without power.

When You Do Have Authority over the Other Person, Make Your Communication Fit Your Leadership Habits

Influencing and commanding are variations on persuading. Think of choosing the fine points of your language according to your position on a spectrum of management "style." That spectrum starts with managers who give their subordinates direct orders and expect obedience. Managers who place more emphasis on the acceptance of their decisions by their associates often start by extolling the advantages and payoffs of what they want. Then they lay out the details of what they want done. Managers who see themselves as still more participative start with a statement of the problem, encourage comment, pro and con, and then say what they want done. Managers who value the total participation of their associates lay out the problem, encourage comment, and then invite their associates to help choose among the available alternatives.

Whichever of those styles you choose, either permanently or according to the situation, requires its own set of verb forms and nonverbals to communicate the final decision effectively. The alternatives include both the mood and the tense of the verb and sometimes the words used to preface the verb. The alternatives are these:

1. The imperative mood is tempting, powerful, and provocative. The word "imperative" comes from "imperator," which is Latin for commander. If you want to give a command with the best chance of the addressee's knowing what you want, use the imperative. That means, speak the verb without any subject. Add an object, a time, or a place if your command needs it to be complete. You are not only giving a command, you are establishing or reinforcing an environment. So fit your tone of voice, facial expression, and body movements to that environment. An example is, "Finish that report by five o'clock!" The exclamation point instead of a period is correct for writing the imperative.

That punctuation, however, does not call for the manager to replace it with nonverbal signals in speaking to a subordinate.

The advantages of the imperative are its brevity, its almost certain understanding by the addressee of what you expect from him, and its strong suggestion that you know what you are doing. For those reasons the imperative and its supporting nonverbals are welcomed by subordinates who are uncertain, in a panic, or otherwise ready to be told what to do.

The disadvantages of the imperative include its likelihood of arousing resentment on the part of subordinates who think they already know what to do or who simply like to be asked rather than told. It also has the disadvantages of encouraging you to see yourself as having to be the critical parent because your subordinates are children. And you may come to like the obedience it derives from some subordinates. You may be tempted to try to reduce the negative impact of the imperative by prefacing it with "please." Don't. "Please" is ideal for asking someone to pass the salt, but in an organizational setting its combination with the imperative is a contradiction in terms and will confuse those who expect you to give orders. Adding the "please" purely as a matter of formality can be inconsistent with reality when tempers have been aroused.

There is another way to avoid the resentment with little sacrifice of brevity or clarity. Preface the imperative with something like, "Here are some suggestions." Communicate from your adult state and address the other person's adult state. That means change your nonverbals to avoid any suggestion through tone of voice or gesture that you are relying on your position or authority.

You can also use the imperative, as I have in this text, to address those over whom you have no organizational control. In such instances, you are submitting your best recommendations as part of an attempt to persuade someone to a course of action, but you are not trying to dictate.

2. The subjunctive mood is not provocative but requires careful grammar. Here are a couple of examples (along with the grammar rules): "I ask that the report be made brief." In the imperative that would read, "Make the report brief." In the subjunctive, the verb "be" replaces the more familiar "is" and "are" of the present tense. The verb "were" replaces "was" in the past tense. As an example, "If this report were brief, I would be done with it by now." The reason for the special verb forms is that the subjunctive is intended to address conditions that may be impossible.

The principal problem with the subjunctive is the frequency with which even skilled speakers forget to change the form of the verb. Moreover, it is still a command. It has the additional handicap of sounding stilted—as if it had been issued from the speaker's parent state and addressed to the listener's child state. For that reason, it is more suited to impressing than expressing.

What does all this mean? It means use the subjunctive to influence only if you are familiar with the rules of grammar and if you are in the small-talk phase of time structuring in which no one takes the conversation seriously. If you are in the problem-solving phase, avoid the subjunctive.

3. The future tense is for official pronouncements. Here's something from a specification: "The sealant will maintain its adhesion to the paint." That language has been used for decades. But if you say, "You will complete the report by five today," fear and/or resentment on the part of the addressee are inevitable. Although the accompanying non-verbals could make that sentence into a question, if it comes from your parent state, it is as much threat as command.

Another problem with using the future tense to give an order is its reversal of the "shall and will" rules of grammar. In the future tense, "I and we" are associated with "shall," and "you, he, she, it, and they" require "will." When the future is used to express determination or to command, those association rules are reversed. If you are stating a specification, make it read, "The contractor shall provide the sealant." If you are talking about something that is going to happen in a matter-of-fact way, use the future tense and don't reverse shall and will. An example is, "I think the contractor will provide the sealant." If you are a manager who is trying to give direction to a subordinate, don't use the future as you would in specification or contract language.

4. A combination of "if" and "then" can influence the addressee through negotiation. A manager can negotiate with a subordinate when he views the subordinate as a client. The manager makes a conditional offer with the intention of having the client feel free to choose. Beguiling. Even though you, the manager, select nonthreatening words and non-verbals, you are still the manager, and the subordinate knows it.

If you want to use this pattern of communication to influence, spend some time assuring the subordinate that he is the client, but be prepared for some unstated disbelief. If you are negotiating with someone on your level or with whom there is no concern over relative authority, the if/then combination can be effective. But it is for bargaining and commits you to giving something in return. Don't be surprised if your subordinates grow to like it and always want to bargain when you try to change their performance.

5. The "potential form of the subjunctive mood" is the most popular. The potential is the name given by grammarians to the use of verbs such as must, should, could, and might to preface a second verb that prescribes the action. The range of choices possible in the first verb allows the speaker to vary the intensity of his desire for change on the part of

the other person. An example of maximum intensity is, "You must finish that report by five." One variation on the potential form is to phrase the request as a question such as, "Would (or could) you finish that report by five?"

Another variation on the potential appends the word "to" to a verb intended to direct. That verb includes have to, ought to, need to, may want to, and dozens of other combinations frequently prefaced by "really" and "very well." An example is, "You might very well want to finish that report by five."

The frequency with which most managers use the potential form suggests that it must have advantages. It has two. It allows the Teddy Roosevelt in us to speak softly but without surrendering our managerial big stick. The manager can see himself as being helpful, rather than masterful. He communicates from his nurturing-parent state while attempting to address the adaptive-child state of the subordinate. On the other hand, the potential form is indirect; it wastes time, and its comparative intensity is easily misunderstood. Don't use it.

6. The indicative mood starts with a preface and then makes a declarative statement. A directive using the indicative mood would read like this: The preface: "Here's the way I see this project operating." The declarative statement: "You finish the report by five." The indicative is even more powerful when the list of declarative statements includes something the boss does as part of the project. It's simple, virtually impossible to misunderstand, and free of threat—other than its having been issued by the boss. The indicative is particularly useful when the manager wants to inform everyone of his role in projects and procedures that require coordinated action by several people. The indicative assumes obedience without prohibiting dissension.

In spite of its obvious advantages, few managers use the indicative when trying to give direction to their subordinates. Why? Because it requires the manager to communicate strictly from his adult state and to address the adult state of the subordinate. That means using words and nonverbals that show equality of purpose, dedication, and rank.

7. Another alternative is to start with "I." This is not a direct extension of the I message from Chapter 5, because it includes your expectation. On the other hand, it does preface the action verb(s) with the first person singular pronoun. An example might be, "I expect you to finish that report by five this evening." It sounds a little like the subjunctive, but uses conventional verbs, because it addresses a possible condition rather than one that may be impossible. The variations in the first verb mean that this means of communicating your wishes offers at least as much variation of intensity of your desire as does the potential form of the subjunctive.

Your directive could also have started with such prefaces as "I prefer,

I would really appreciate, I need, I am asking, I would like, I will expect, I insist, I demand, or I must have." The list is long.

Like self-disclosure (Chapter 5), this method can reduce threat by avoiding the use of "you" or its other forms. "I expect to have the finished report by five this evening." Couple it with complementary nonverbals, and your message becomes even clearer.

An "I need" message may be so clear to you that you conclude that feedback is unnecessary. No message is received that clearly. If the addressee doesn't give you feedback, ask for it with "I need some feedback on what I just said." And follow up with a request for a status report at 4:30. The benefits of "I need" and its variations include its allowing you to inject yourself as a person into the directive.

Its chief advantage is that it allows you to be nonthreatening and polite and to avoid giving a direct order. Its grammar is straightforward. You can even open with a general statement, "I need help—by five PM— from you." In most cases you will have the undivided attention of the subordinate.

Use this form when the adult ego state is in charge or when you think you may have overused other verb forms. The "I need" method has its problems. You may couple it with the passive voice thinking that you are reducing threat even more. Maybe; but the passive either conceals information about the source of the action or uses extra words. An example is, "I need that report to be completed by five today." By whom? You could add, "by you," but why waste the words? There are some other disadvantages. If you use it every time you give a directive, it will sound repetitious. It also allows the addressee who doesn't know your habits to assume your need is not critical, when in fact it is. It is highly sensitive to your nonverbal signals. Check your ego state and your estimate of the capabilities of the other person before you phrase the "I need," and choose the verb that most accurately meets your needs as a manager. Be careful not to slip into "we," when you mean "you."

Avoid the Risks Inherent with the Skills

The better you become at persuasion or at direction, the more power you will have over the actions of others. Consider first those over whom you have no authority but whom you have persuaded to take a certain action. As your reputation grows, you will earn additional assignments in which you are expected to convince others of the advantages of adopting a new system. If the system you proposed fails to live up to expectations, you will be accused of having oversold it. You may be accused of having presented only part of the vital data. You may be seen by your fellow technical managers as having "abandoned your technical dignity."

You have entered the least attractive of all organizational worlds. You have inherited accountability without having had the authority at any point in the process. If it went poorly, a poorly trained supervisor will try to blame you. If it succeeded, your having persuaded without power means you have lived up to Lao Tsu's prescription for the ideal leader. Lao Tsu taught the saying: "As for the best leaders, the people do not notice their existence. The next best, the people honor and praise. The next, the people fear, and the next, the people hate. When the best leader's work is done the people say, 'we did it ourselves.' "

With so many personal risks associated with being successful at persuasion without power, you might decide to leave it to someone else. Most technically trained managers do. This is understandable, but it is career limiting for the manager and profit limiting for the firm, especially when the technical manger is uniquely qualified by his knowledge.

The risks associated with success in persuasion merit some countermeasures. For one, keep a careful record of every time you to go into the persuade-without-power mode. Write your account as if you had been handed a basket of lemons, but you made lemonade. In every case, make sure you point out how your actions helped the organization and furthered your boss's career. Technically trained managers who are adept at persuasion are always in demand in consulting, in design, in manufacturing, and in technical sales. In addition to keeping your own record, report your accomplishment to your boss, and do it so as to reflect favorably on his performance, as well.

Consider now those whom you persuaded and over whom you had authority. You may be feeling so good because of what you have accomplished that you can't wait to go tell someone. But don't leave or change the subject until you have heard satisfactory feedback with no conflicting nonverbals.

Assume now that the persuasion is long past, and the subordinate has started to do what you ask. Chapter 10 includes a discussion of potential problem analysis. No matter how well you communicated when you made the assignment, there is always the possibility that something unpredicted by either you or the subordinate can happen. Think it through, and if it is likely, prepare a contingency plan.

The Rewards

Build with your associates a reputation for persuading without power or the threat of it and you can reach a workable compromise with them quickly when speed is necessary. Your reputation for persuasion without threat or power will generate a lasting trust of you and your motives by those who report to you. Your superiors will come to depend on you to persuade representatives of outside groups to accept your group's position. Even in those instances when you don't have the time to move through all the elements of persuasion, rejection, apparent or real, will not defeat you. In fact, you will use those rejections to help redirect your approach. The uncertainties associated with persuading someone else to change will never go away, but you will feel confident of your ability to see that they are resolved.

Fit the Skills to Yourself and Your Job

If you are persuading someone over whom you have organizational power, choose your verbs according to:

1. The balance of power between you and the receiver.
2. The verb combinations you like to have others use with you. A caution here: some "others" will not always respond to a verb combination as you do.
3. What you may have to put in writing later.
4. Your personal-preferences relative to the pros and cons of each technique.

Patience Gains Acceptance by Associates

The volume of material in this chapter are sufficient to merit your careful re-reading and practice in private before you use these methods of persuading. Don't broadcast what you are doing; just do it. If anyone asks what you're up to, answer in terms of how objectives are set and what you do to accomplish them. Stay away from the theory, and don't mention any of the techniques by name. If anyone recognizes the techniques, let them bring up the names.

A Problem for You to Solve

"I know they would be a lot better off if they would use the program I designed."

My name is Timsen; I am a program analyst and designer. I have put together a program that will make life a lot easier for users of local area networks (LANs). I have had some professional help in working up a neat presentation for the managers of several groups that use LANs. The two managers to whom I have given the presentation have listened politely enough but then have put out all sorts of reasons why they couldn't adopt the program. For instance, one of them objected to the program on the grounds of its taking more time to install than his department could afford. That was strange, because in the presentation I had pointed out how little time it would take. So I said something to the effect that maybe I wasn't too clear and rehashed that part of the presentation. It didn't help. He promised to think it over and call me, but I haven't heard a word.

Cross-References within This Book

Before you start planning to persuade someone to make a significant change, go back to Chapter 4 and review reflective statements and open-ended questions.

A Problem Solved

"I know they would be a lot better off if they would use the program I designed."

Timsen's problems are typical of those encountered by the technically trained individual who is conscientiously trying to change, for the better, what others are doing. He knows he is right and he knows they would be better off for having adopted his plan. What he doesn't know is that he will either learn to listen to his clients' objections or continue to fail to persuade.

References

Opdyce, John B. *Harper's English Grammar*. Harper and Row, New York, 1965.
"The Engineering of Agreement," 2d ed., Roundtable Films, Beverly Hills, California, 1978.
Lao Tsu, in Fitzhenry, Robert I. *Barnes and Nobel Book of Quotations*. Barnes and Noble Books, New York, 1987.

10

Most of Any Decisionmaking Process Is Communication

Most books on management offer advice on how to make decisions. Some of those books even include a stepwise discipline for solving problems or unraveling mysteries. Kepner and Treoge's *The Rational Manager* offers disciplines for both solving problems and making decisions. In more recent years the authors have developed their method further and have included a chapter on situation appraisal in their successor book, *The New Rational Manager*. This chapter is a guide to selecting the most effective communication skills for use in the current version of K-T (short for the Kepner-Tregoe System). Reflecting one of the values of the new edition, every chapter in this book includes a section entitled, "Appraise the Situation."

Appraise the Situation

K-T consists of four distinct phases. Those phases are situation appraisal, problem analysis, decision analysis, and potential problem analysis. It may sound complicated, but the system works. How well it works, however, depends not only on knowing how and when to use it, but on the skills in interpersonal communication of the people involved, particularly the manager. The communication skills that are of the most value in K-T are assertion (chapter 3), active listening (chapter 4), nonverbal communication (chapter 5), and the exchange of facts (chapter 7). The balance you achieve among those communication skills will do more than increase your chances of making good decisions. That balance will also govern the kinds and degrees of participation you develop among your associates.

K-T starts most effectively with situation appraisal. It asks, "Where are we now?" Situation appraisal invites you to consider your opportunities and your concerns. (You might prefer to express those feelings as hopes or fears.) Among your concerns may be things that puzzle you, things that are not going according to plan, or things that may turn sour over time. Situation appraisal encourages you to state your concerns or opportunities as questions that start with, "why," "how to" or "what if." Situation appraisal then asks you to assign priorities to each question according to its overall rating. That rating consists of subordinate ratings derived from three other questions, which are "how critical," "how urgent," and "growth potential."

Situation appraisal will lead you to problem analysis if the highest priority question starts with a "why." As it leads you to an answer, problem analysis has you compare what you had hoped for with what is actually happening, quantify the difference, look for changes and distinctions, use them to postulate causes for the difference, and select the most probable cause. The end point of problem analysis is the most likely underlying cause for the difference between the intended and the actual. The identification of the cause may indicate a need for a solution to a problem or a chance to take advantage of an opportunity. Either one leads to decision analysis.

On the other hand, situation appraisal leads you directly to decision analysis if the highest priority question starts with "how to." Decision analysis has you set forth objectives, asks you to generate alternative courses of action, asks what new problems might ensure from pursuing each alternative, and presents you with a roughly quantitative way to choose the best alternative.

Your use of situation appraisal may also conclude with the question that start with "what if." The K-T phase known as potential problem analysis was designed to answer such questions. Problem analysis asks you to view an existing situation that seems to be going well and to speculate on the things that might go wrong. It then asks you either to decide what you will do if those things do go wrong or what you will do to reduce the chances that they might.

In spite of the proven and extraordinary value of the problem analysis and potential problem analysis techniques of K-T, both of them are less popular with managers in for-profit organizations than is decision analysis. The difference in popularity may not be too hard to understand when you think that decision analysis starts with a how-to questions and that most decision makers see their primary responsibility as knowing "how to" make things happen.

K-T can be used either by an individual, or by a group, or by an individual with some selective help from a group. Since its usual end point is a selection among alternatives for getting something done, there is a problem of obtaining concurrence with the decision by those persons whose activities are essential to its success. The chances of concurrence will decrease if those who must help it succeed are neither allowed to contribute to its development nor consulted before the decision becomes final. Another source of problem behavior is on the part of those whose freedom of action will be reduced by the decision.

As managing engineer, you may choose to point out that you do not have the time to consult everyone in the organization who might be affected by a decision. Taking advantage of that "right" is almost guaranteed to add to the total time required for broad implementation.

Set the Objectives

The primary objective in the communication associated with K-T or with any decisionmaking discipline will be to choose the verbal and nonverbal skills that match your objectives. Those objectives may change during the situation appraisal, but your job is not only to make a good decision, but to communicate so as to realize the full potential of the method.

You will have organizational criteria to meet, such as time, cost, and product performance. You will have personal criteria to consider, because everyone who participates in this process will need to be treated as important and as capable.

You will have the opportunity to optimize participation in seeking causes, generating alternative courses of action, and in imagining what things might go wrong. You can halt the participative phase at that point and make the final decision yourself. You can also join the rest of the group and become a participant yourself as the group selects the most likely course of action. The more you choose to rely on the group, the more will be your need for patience and self-control.

Another worthwhile objective for you will be the delicate task of encouraging creativity when you try to conjure up possible reasons for a failure or generate possible courses of action. Even as you commence with situation appraisal, make one of your objectives the exploration, or at least the mention, of all significant facts or concerns known to those who are present.

Select the Effective Mental State

To start with, get into the adult ego state and aim your communication at the adult state of those others who are present. Give information, receive concerns, record facts, and avoid communicating from your parent state, even in situations where you have more authority and are convinced that your knowledge is technically superior to that of others present. Follow the rules that you may have come to associate with brainstorming, and do not disagree with or criticize anyone's suggestion. To the best of your ability, make sure no one else criticizes or evaluates negatively any idea that has come from someone in the group. There may come a time to use your nurturing-parent state if someone in the group seems to have a worthwhile contribution, but has difficulty in finding just the right words to express it so others can understand. A constructive step in such a case would be for you to do some rephrasing and then carefully check out your version with the author.

Choose the Skills to Attain the Objectives

Your first job is to become totally familiar with the K-T. Your second job is to refresh yourself with the tools of interpersonal communication that have already appeared in this book.

Situation appraisal is most effective when it is a combination of the expression of facts and the feelings or emotions that are related to those facts. If you are conducting this part of K-T in the presence of a group, it is easily possible for someone to get into their critical-parent role and phrase either facts or feelings, or both, in such ways as to arouse a negative reaction on the part of someone else. As the manager, it is your job not to attack the aggressor, but to restate what he has said in a way that is neutral and concentrates objectively upon the problem, rather than the personalities involved.

Near the end of situation appraisal, you will be involved in assigning priorities to the concerns you have previously listed. Make those assignments on the basis of, admittedly, arbitrary ratings of each concern, according to the standards previously discussed. You will often find that members of the group will disagree strongly on the priorities assigned to the various "why," "how to," and "what if" questions. Careful objective discussion will reduce the range of priorities. You may even have to settle for an average to develop a most likely priority for the next step in K-T method. If you have a handy spread sheet or a K-T program for your microcomputer, it can help resolve differences.

There is another alternative. You can carefully and objectively explore with each party to the discussion the reasons behind the priorities he has favored. Your best communication skills, at this point, are the open-ended question and active listening. If you attempt to push for an answer, you will obtain the answer, but it will probably bear little resemblance to the underlying truth. Through careful listening and restating, you have a much better chance of developing the real cause for someone's position. Once you know the cause, your chances of achieving a productive resolution of differences of priority are much greater.

Assume you have successfully passed the situation appraisal hurdle and that the priorities have led you into problem analysis. This was the phase of K-T that first made the method popular. Inevitably you will find that, in some groups, there will be a tendency to jump to a premature decision on what has been causing the problem. Some of the time, those jumps are correct; most are not. On the contrary, any problem that is of such significance that it took first priority in situation appraisal will not be one that is solved by a hip-shot approach. This is a time when you will have to listen both for facts and for feelings. There will be some present who may feel very nervous about the exploration of changes that have been made in a process or a material, because such changes may lead to a distinction that suggests a cause. Their nervousness will be associated with the possibility that the change was their idea. Again, your most effective communication skill is the open-ended question. Keep asking "what," "why," and "how" until you are satisfied that all of the relevant data are at hand. If you find that one of the persons present made a decision that seems to be at the heart of the problem, do not use the occasion to judge that person's action or intentions. The purposes of problem analysis are to decide what is the cause of a problem and prepare for the succeeding decision analysis, which will do something to remedy it. The purposes of problem analysis do not include any form of verbal or nonverbal punishment of the offending party by your communicating from your critical-parent state.

If you have been as skillful in your communication as in the use of the technique up to this point, the emotional barriers to finding a solution should have been overcome.

Your having overcome those emotional aspects will be particularly valuable as the group starts to cite objectives for whatever course of action is chosen and then subdivides those objectives into "musts" and "wants." Write each "must" objective so that everyone will understand how it is to be measured. Assign to each "want" objective a weight (a number from one through nine, for example) and make sure everyone present understands these weights will be used later to help select among the courses of action that have already satisfied the "must" objectives. There will be disagreement, but don't let it evade the need for careful, factual establishment of those weights.

When the weights have been established, make sure everyone present understands that the final selection of a course of action will be based on its ability to pass the "musts" and to do well against the weighted "wants." The selection will not be made on the basis of a debate of the strong and weak factors of each alternative after those alternatives have been identified.

Now, develop the alternatives. Seek objectivity, but recognize that political and personal agendas may hinder it. If by using your neutral, objective adult state and listening you have established a trust among the rest of the group, the effects of the personal and political aspects will be minimized.

The next to the last step in decision analysis is to list the potential adverse consequences for each of the courses of action that still survive. Again, there is an opportunity for subjective differences to appear. By this time, you may have exceeded your capacity for resolving differences by listening and restating, and it may be time to take a break. When you come back, the objective will not have changed; it is still to obtain rational statements of what might go wrong with each of the alternatives. The last step is to select the most attractive alternative that has passed all of the "must" objectives and rates the highest on a weighted basis against the "want" objectives.

You may find in your organization that the K-T phase known as potential problem analysis is not popular. Neither are boat-rockers nor prophets of doom. They provide a service, however, by reminding the rest of us that the plans of mice and men don't always succeed. There will inevitably be a tendency at this point to react to the suggestion of a potential problem with a communication from the negative adaptive-child, which may threaten the cohesion of the group. Fortunately, this phase of K-T is useful in situations where the decisions have all been made and where, perhaps, there has been a change of the guard in management. The group that is concerned about potential problems will consider what can happen, what is the probability that it might go wrong, and how damaging it would be. To answer those questions effectively, communicate from your adult state. If indeed the situation is one in which those who are doing this analysis are different from the group that made the original decision, be alert for communications that issue from the critical parent state, and attack the legacy of the previous group. Hear them out, but restate them as if they had come from the adult state.

Preparations for solving a potential problem can be made in either of two ways. One is to agree that little of consequence can be done now, but that if the problem occurs, a pre-arranged plan will be followed to solve it. A second approach is to take steps now to minimize, if not completely erase, the chances of damage from the potential problem, should it occur. The communication skills that are of the greatest value in anticipating a potential problem are those of the little-professor ego state. That means use your imagination to create a range of actions, and let financial or technical conditions help select the most attractive.

Avoid the Risks Inherent with the Skills

No matter what the temptation or any attempt at coercion by some members of the group, do not allow your words or your nonverbal signals to suggest that you are abdicating your part in any of the phases in K-T method. Be prepared for a negative reaction to the active listening that has served you so well in K-T. Some of your associates who are unfamiliar with active listening or who have never seen it properly used will see it as a sign of weakness on your part. In the extreme, they may also see you as abdicating your role in the decisionmaking process. To avoid that problem, discipline your nonverbal transmissions so that you do not give any suggestion of wanting to avoid your obligations as a manager.

A risk inherent in your having avoided the traditionally managerial critical-parent role is that some of the group members will decide you are fair game for venting their frustrations. If they do, you have several alternatives. One is to use the fogging technique described in Chapter 3 and to keep using it until the frustrated group members exhaust their criticisms. Another is to reflect the frustration and try to identify its source as part of the reflection. Still another is to call a break and take the frustrated group member aside for the purpose of delivering an I message. Do that only if the expressions of frustration have caused a significant loss of time or group cohesion, as well as having been offensive to you personally.

The Rewards

A combination of the skills of interpersonal communication with those of K-T is a virtual guarantee that the decisions you and your group make will be effective. Further, your having encouraged creativity (in the little-professor ego state) in the problem and decision analysis phases of K-T will send a clear signal that you value creativity in such other aspects of the group's activity as product and process design.

Fit the Skills to Yourself and to Your Job

You may find yourself in an organization in which participative decisionmaking is given no more than lip service. Having helped make a decision that came out of the group, you may find you will have to convince your boss of three things. One is that the decision was a wise one. Another is that your communication techniques and the broad use of your group paid off in the quality of the decision and justified the time it took. The third is that your decision style didn't "give away the store" to your subordinates.

Do not leave a decisionmaking meeting thinking that verbal concurrence means whole-hearted cooperation. It does not. No matter how careful you have been about your communications, there will be some present who later decided they did not get a fair opportunity to speak or that none of the ideas that survived in the final decision were theirs and, therefore, they have little obligation to carry out the group decision.

Patience Gains Acceptance by Associates

Group decisionmaking may have such a bad name in your organization that, no matter what your intentions, it will be seen by others as manipulative or as a means for you to "hide behind a group." If you are accused of either of these actions, you have several defenses. One is to say nothing and let the results of your group's decisions speak for you. Another is to invite your accusers to sit with the group the next time they go through a K-T exercise, having suggested that the visit might give them a different idea of what you are trying to accomplish. The possibility of your being accused of having abdicated your responsibility as a manager has already been mentioned.

Should you find yourself in a forum in which you can discuss that suggestion unemotionally, propose to the rest that a manager can delegate power, can delegate duty or obligation, can delegate credit for something well done, but cannot delegate the blame for something that went wrong. Your acceptance of that final accountability may do more to set you apart from some of the other managers than to explain your philosophy of management, but it will be unquestionably accepted and understood by those who report to you.

One more suggestion: If the risks associated with participative decisionmaking appear to be unacceptably high, do a potential problem analysis on your own situation. It may give you some ideas about how to report the results of the decisionmaking process to your immediate superior, both orally and in writing.

Problems for You to Solve

First Among Equals

Don Methinyl prides himself in opening meetings of his project team with several comments that outline his perference for involving everyone in major decisions. He frequently states his belief in the values of participative management both in development of his subordinates and in achieving the schedule and financial goals of the project. When he is extolling the virtues of his approach, he stands at the head of the conference table or walks around it and leans over each team member while making a point. One of the things he sees as a benefit of his interest in participative decisionmaking is the generally low incidence of quarrels among the members of his project team when a decision is made. His team does not always finish projects on schedule, but Methinyl attributes this fact to the amount of time it takes to let everyone feel their viewpoint is equal in value to that of everyone else.

For the past few years, the organization has been operating on loose schedules, so no one has worried about Methinyl's slow pace. About six months ago, however, a new director of engineering came in from another part of the firm. He has spoken twice with Methinyl and has been very critical. Methinyl has thought it all over and has about decided that he should be less participative. He plans to start at tomorrow's team meeting and make it clear that he is in charge and that, while he wants advice, he makes the decisions.

We're All in This Together

Teanor has been a supervising engineer in a large manufacturing firm for three years. He is even sharper on economic analyses now than when he was promoted. He works very hard and is generally liked but not highly respected. He had over five years to watch his boss make decisions and to observe the boss's communication practices that went along with the decisions. He watched as his boss was given two promotions without ever seeming to make the final decision about anything. Teanor liked the way his boss handled decisionmaking situations and made sure everyone had his say. His boss often said, "I may be the supervisor, but we're all involved in this."

When he was promoted, Teanor was sure the way his boss operated was the only way. Within the last three months he has become aware of some not-too-subtle hints by his subordinates that he may be "hiding behind the group." He has come to you for help. You are one of his peers.

Kinda-Sorta

Jeremy knows how to make decisions. He has even written a few letters to the editor of the local newspaper criticizing the haphazard way the city council decides things, especially those having to do with expenditures. He has been an engineering manager for enough years to know what has to be done to implement such decisions as changing the quality assurance system for a new product line. He prides himself in his style of communicating a decision to the person who will do most of the work. That style has served him well, especially in instances where the tasks involved in carrying out the decision were difficult or unattractive.

Jeremy has learned to convey the instruction in terms that include the least possible amount of authority. Those terms are "kinda" and "sorta." He always prefaces a directive with one or both of those contractions.

He speaks slowly and has a naturally soft voice, both of which go well with his phraseology. An example is, "Would you kinda redesign that phase switch and sorta reduce the manufactured cost to half its present value?"

The theory is admirable: Insert a phrase that softens the impact of a difficult assignment. The problem arises in its implementation. Some of Jeremy's people are new in the division, and they are puzzled by what seems to be a contradiction. They think Jeremy knows what he would like to see happen, but they aren't sure he really expects them to do it. As a result, some things aren't being done on time, and some not at all. Jeremy sees both failures as a lack of appreciation for his carefully honed communication style and is increasingly disappointed with the performances of his newer people.

Problems Solved

First among Equals

If Methinyl goes through with his intention of letting everyone know who is in charge, his team members will probably welcome the congruency between what he says and his body language. His problem to date has been that his standing over people while telling them of his liking of participative decisionmaking has left them believing the nonverbal component. As a result, his communication has defeated his objective. If he believes in participative decisionmaking as much as he says he does, he would be better off to have someone in the training department videotape him at the next meeting so he could see how his body language was contrasting with his words.

We're All in This Together

Teanor is stretching so far in the direction of letting everyone have his say that he doesn't bring the decisionmaking process to a close. Teanor is sending the message that he wants to hear all viewpoints. He is not, however, sending the message that part of his job is to see that a decision is made. In all likelihood, he is also failing to remind his subordinates that while he is a part of the decision, he alone has the accountability for the results, especially if they are negative.

Kinda-Sorta

Carl Rogers urged us to be clear and congruent when expressing our feelings about what someone has done in a critical session. Jeremy is neither clear nor congruent in communicating directions. If there is hope for him, it may come from someone's experiencing a critical failure because Jeremy told someone to "kinda" do something. And that someone assumed Jeremy was neither serious nor specific when in fact he was both. If the injured party confronts Jeremy with a carefully worded "I Message" as in Chapter 5, Jeremy may find a more precise term than "kinda." There is another possibility. Let's say Jeremy complains to someone who actively listens while Jeremy lists his gripes about his subordinates' casual performance. There is an old saying, "How do I know what I think until I hear what I say?" Jeremy may come to realize that his communication style is the culprit, not his subordinates' lack of interest.

References

Kepner, Charles H., and Benjamin B. Tregoe. *The New Rational Manager*. Kepner-Tregoe, Princeton, New Jersey, 1981,

Kepner, Charles H., and Benjamin B. Tregoe. *The Rational Manager*. Kepner-Tregoe, Inc. Princeton, New Jersey, 1965.

11

The More Communication, the Better the Performance Planning

The primary intention of this chapter is for you to learn how to apply some of the interpersonal communication skills of previous chapters when you are the appraiser. This chapter also provides you with applications of those skills from the viewpoint of the appraisee. You will be exposed to the differences in the communication patterns among several appraisal philosophies. You will see that some of those philosophies don't merit the use of terms like "appraisal" or "review."

This chapter does not intend to instruct you in how to set up a complete system of performance planning. By its title, however, it suggests that the usual pattern of praise, punish, or postpone will not appear. This chapter will emphasize the roles of feedback and their advantages to appraisee and appraiser. That feedback will be both invited and uninvited. It will emphasize the present and the future rather than the past.

These communication skills will help you to manage and perhaps to motivate but not to manipulate those whose performance you are expected to review. These skills will accommodate the official system, but will not try to change it. You will derive some ideas on how to audit the communication practices you use in the appraisal process and those used by managers subordinate to you.

Appraise the Situation

Most engineers in management will postpone the annual interviews as long as they can and may have to be coerced into giving them. And when they do meet with their subordinates, they talk too much. Veteran appraisees often say very little but usually send many nonverbals.

The managers don't talk nearly enough during the year or so that leads up to the annual interview. They forget, dismiss as inappropriate, or avoid at all costs chances during the performance period to use communication to develop their subordinates. Those omissions can be associated with either desirable or undesirable performance. In either case, the year-end interview is usually so long after the fact as to render both compliments and criticisms nearly worthless in terms of future improvements of performance. It's always too late for the appraisee to do anything about performance that is being reviewed.

Part of managing the communication in any appraisal process is assessing its worth. In most organizations, the appraisal process itself is seldom, if ever, evaluated. When it is, the cause is usually some extraordinary act by an employee or in response to a lawsuit.

The organization's attitude toward the appraisal system is mixed. On one hand, convincing engineering managers to conduct performance appraisals is the bane of the human resources director's existence. On the other hand, the regulations associated with equal employment opportunity require that records of performance review of certain classes of employees be kept. You could probably predict that those who are primarily concerned about keeping the organization out of trouble will emphasize proper completion of the official form over how well the appraisee does his job during the next appraisal period.

The mental state of the appraisee encompasses the most variety of any of the factors surrounding the appraisal system. It is usually negative. He comes in with a chip on his shoulder and signals it nonverbally. If he has been around for a few years, he has had many disappointments. Early in his career he was eager to hear how well he did in the last year or so. He came into the interview in the most hopeful adaptive-child ego state. His boss, however, was so uncomfortable with the process that all he wanted to do was have the appraisee read what he had written, sign the form, and go on to something more related to engineering. The boss failed to sense the mental state of the appraisee and gave only lip service to the whole thing.

The appraisee learned a lesson. He learned that management is something that can hurt people. Callouses formed. Before long the appraisee was in the same mode as that of the manager: Let's get it over with.

The picture isn't all bad. Some managers have learned the value of meeting once a month or at least once every three months. They have applied that learning not only to their subordinates but to their bosses.

Set the Objectives

When You Are the Appraiser

Fix firmly in your mind that your job is to concentrate on performance—not the person. You are under certain organizational constraints, but the majority of your actions surrounding the process are under your control. Make some basic assumptions about the philosophy of appraisals and appraisal interviews that you want to follow. For example, decide if you believe that projection and planning help performance more than review and appraisal. Admit that no one likes to play God, so that your trepidations are not unique to you. Review the styles of interviewing in the section of this chapter titled "Choose the Skills to Attain the Objectives," and choose the one that best fits your objectives.

Render unto Caesar the things that are Caesar's. That means being prepared to observe the communication demands of whatever system the organization prefers. For example, if the organization has a strict policy against discussing salary during the interview, be prepared to observe it. Later you can observe the organizational rules of timing with respect to announcing salary adjustments.

Decide in advance if you will communicate to help yourself motivate the appraisee or manage his future performance. If you choose to try to motivate, decide what you mean by that term and how you will know if your communication is successful. If you prefer to manage for future performance, decide in advance if you want the interview to produce a joint statement of objectives, activities, or a combination that will guide the next interview. If you prefer to manage by exception and review performance only on that basis, decide if you will emphasize positive performance, failure, or both.

If the organization sets a specific schedule for appraisal reviews, decide in advance if you will wait until the end of the period before you bring up questions of performance. If that arrangement won't meet your needs, write an algorithm that will decide for you when to have an interview with your subordinates. Include in that algorithm a provision for treating them all alike.

When You Are the Appraisee

Make your primary objective that of not surprising the boss with any last minute confessions or goodies. As a secondary objective, decide that you will avoid fight or flight in reaction to negative comments from the boss and what reaction you will prefer. Have a pre-made decision to guide your reaction to comments that relate to you as a person rather than to your performance. Have a schedule in advance for when you will draft a personal development plan or a revision of the old one and when you will seek feedback on it from the boss.

Select the Effective Mental State

When You Are the Appraiser

Your critical-parent ego state is ideal for the introductory small talk, but don't enter any exchange about the firm's appraisal review practices. If you prefer a style of interview in which you "tell it like it is," communicate from your critical-parent state, but confine your comment to actions and their effects on the organization and your job. Think of the appraisee not as a child to be spanked, but as an adult who is capable of reacting constructively to hearing the results of his performance from his boss. Don't think in terms of praise or punishment.

If a disagreement should arise or if the appraisee should become emotional, switch into your adult state and use active listening until the tensions are gone.

You may prefer a style of interview in which you tell the appraisee what changes in his performance you expect and then try to sell him on the advantages of meeting your wishes. That style will require you either to use your positive, adaptive-child state, to "sell up," or your adult state, to exchange feelings and facts until the appraisee sells himself.

If at the end of the interview you want to include a feedback exchange with the appraisee, use your adult role until the two of you have a common understanding at least of the more significant points.

When You Are the Appraisee

Your critical-parent state is ideal for the introductory small talk, but only if your boss is comfortable with that way of leading into the more formal aspects. If you have received a compliment and you like what you heard, your positive natural-child state is ideal. If either you personally or your performance has been criticized, think and communicate from your adult state and use the coping skills from Chapter 3 until the criticism stops. If the personal elements survive the interview, use your adult role in an attempt to engage the appraiser in a comparison of facts and their interpretations. Do not, no matter what the provocation, slip into roller derby or flight via your adaptive-child.

Choose the Skills to Attain the Objectives

When You Are the Appraiser—Before the Interview

Start the day after the last interview to prepare for the next one. Assume and plan for an interview that will be more valuable to the appraisee and to the organization because you and he cover all recent, pertinent information. Plan to use self-disclosure to communicate to the subordinate the results of his more significant efforts as soon as possible after those results are clear. Whether the efforts and their results are positive or negative, they merit your quantitative analysis and prompt expression. Practice formulating and giving both critical and complimentary I messages during the period leading up to the interview.

Once you are relieved of the stress of the interview, you will have a natural tendency to let down and to rely on the next one to make your points. When the appraisee has done something significant to the general good, don't use excuses such as, "That is what we pay people for," to justify your omitting or delaying giving him a positive self-disclosure report.

Don't let a corporate phobia for conversation about anything unpleasant prevent your giving a negative self-disclosure report. Instead, carefully formulate and practice delivering a negative I message; give it, and seek feedback to be sure it was received accurately. Next ask for a plan and a schedule to improve that particular performance.

Make part of your planning the choice of a "style" which will guide your communication during the interview. Use the material below to choose a style that you think best fits you, the appraisee, and the situation.

If you find yourself wanting to use the word"you" when covering a negative part of performance, re-read Chapter 5 and learn how to comment on what he did, not on him. If you still want to use that word, it means you want to punish or get even. Before you go any further, switch to self-confrontation and dredge up whatever is at the bottom of your motivation.

Your firm may have an appraisal system that calls for you to meet with each of your subordinates every twelve months, having filled out a form in advance and having received one from the appraisee. Your objectives for your own performance planning system may not be served by such a long interval or even by a fixed interval. In fact, your system may work best if a random number generator sets the dates. In the next series of interviews review your objectives with each of your subordinates and propose a higher frequency. You may need to achieve a workable compromise, but it will have the participative support of most of your associates.

Present and Persuade

Present the facts of the appraisee's performance and their effects as you know them. That means prepare for the interview by compiling a written list of short I messages. Arrange the room so you and the appraisee can sit side-by-side and look at the list together. Some of the items will usually speak to problems and some to successes. Whether positive or negative, make your I messages obey the doctrine of "clear and congruent (honest)." Don't try to use the "sandwich" technique, by which you insert something unpleasant between two slices of good-tasting bread. That method may work for feeding a baby who has a discriminating sense of taste, but it is counterproductive in a performance interview.

Prepare also a schedule and a plan for the results and perhaps some specific actions you expect from him during the next performance period. Be prepared with defensible reasons why you expect the performance. Include in your plan a time for recapitulation of what is said and enough feedback for you to be sure he knows what you want. Plan to concentrate on facts and actions, but not to involve any active listening.

Present, Question, Listen, and Plan

As with "Present and Persuade," write the list of I messages. But this time prepare a list of questions—some open-ended and some directive—that will elicit any ideas the appraisee has about what to do next. Listen for facts, not feelings. If the appraisee brings up emotional aspects of a given task, or resists the whole idea, be prepared to switch to active listening and to stay there until he has had his say.

Have a performance plan for him that contains only the results you expect. He may want to debate the feasibility of some of the results. Be prepared, therefore, to allow him to plan the activities that should produce the results you want, but not to decide on the results themselves. A feedback plan is the last step.

Listen, Present, and Plan

Prepare yourself to listen to whatever concerns the appraisee. Have a list of results you want him to accomplish. Work with him to develop a parallel list of activities for him to pursue to achieve the results. Finish up with feedback.

Listen without Structure and Ask for a Plan

This approach calls for you only to prepare yourself to listen for facts and feelings. It allows the appraisee to choose the topics and say anything he wants. After the listening, help him prepare a plan to resolve his concerns and yours. If you reach the end of the process and you still have some concerns about his performance, state them as I messages and modify the plan accordingly. Plan for a feedback session at the end.

When You Are the Appraiser—During the Interview

Except for those cases where you select the "Present and Persuade" method, encourage the subordinate to express his hopes and fears for his performance during the coming period or even far beyond it. On the other hand, do not encourage any revelations from the appraisee that even border on the personal.

One of the dangers of being a good active listener is that your unquestioning acceptance of whatever the appraisee says will encourage him to disclose personal things. The appraisee will come away with a permanent fear that you may reveal that information or use it to his disadvantage.

As you and the appraisee cover his plans for the coming period, give him enough feedback for both of you to be sure what he will do during that period. If he has revealed anything of a personal nature, comment on it in a general way and say that you will make no paper, electronic, or mental record of it.

If the appraisee has expressed hopes about his performance or his career, let him know you are open to such discussions and give him enough feedback for him to know that he made his point and that you will think it through and let him know later what you will do about it.

In many cases he will bring up desires that are beyond your authority to grant. Compare his hopes with what you know to be organizational reality. While he may already know the limits of your authority, it's time for the exchange of the facts of the matter, but solely on an adult-to-adult basis. His questions may sound as if they came from his adaptive-child state, but that is no excuse for your to communicate from your parent state.

When You Are the Appraiser—After the Interview

Ask the appraisee to write down what he thinks the two of you have said and to have it on your desk by the end of the next day. Make sure his activities and objectives agree with your concept and that you meet your part of the follow-up schedule.

When You Are the Appraisee—Before the Interview

Your boss may never have learned the art of self-disclosure. He may prefer to talk all around a sore point but never to come to grips with it. He may also be capable of communicating only from the parent ego state in a stressful situation and resort to accusations or implications of inadequate performance on your part. If the latter is the case, review and practice the coping skills of assertion: They are described in Chapter 3. If you have already adopted the 3-P (Progress, Plans, and Proposals) form of reporting, base your preparation on those reports. If not, refer to the upcoming section, "The Rewards" and start using that system now.

When You Are the Appraisee—During the Interview

If the boss implies or accuses you of a transgression and you know you are innocent, it is time for one of the forms of acknowledging. Don't agree with him and don't challenge him. Ask for some time to think it over and dig up the facts later. You may find that when you meet with him later he has abandoned the attack. If not, state your point, present your documentation, and shut up about it.

If the accusation is accurate, it's time for negative assertion. That means if you have already covered it in a 3-P report, agree with what he says and let it go at that. If you haven't already reported on it, agree with him, admit your embarrassment or however you feel, and stop.

If on careful reflection you don't see the significance of the act, consider asking him why all the fuss. That's negative inquiry. If you have any reason to think that he may see your question as a challenge to his authority, don't use it. Instead, use manageable concerns and ask his advice on how to remedy the situation or how to avoid making the same error again.

When You Are the Appraisee—After the Interview

Create your own written plan for "management by your activities and the boss's objectives." When you have reduced it to the fewest possible words, phase it into the next 3-P report and ask for his feedback.

Count yourself fortunate if your boss has carefully fashioned constructive combinations of communication skills for performance interviews. If he has not, count yourself among the majority and start after the next interview to do something about it.

Avoid the Risks Inherent with the Skills

If you feel a desire to compare your communication pattern in performance interviews with those of other managers, wait until they ask. The word will spread quickly among the appraisees. They will eventually tell their bosses. The bosses will feel a little uncomfortable about the situation and will want to know what you are doing. Give them the facts, but don't try to convince anyone of the virtues of what you do.

Make sure they all understand that you are honoring the requirements of the firm.

The Rewards

The time you need to spend next year overseeing your appraisees' performance will decrease in proportion to their and your participation in this year's interviews. Their performance levels will rise. If the style you adopt includes active listening, they will learn that they can trust you. If your style includes I messages, they will learn to expect complete honesty from you. You may even find you have some new connections to the corporate grapevine.

Somehow find a place on the boss's calendar and schedule a meeting with him at least once a month. Don't count the chance meetings in the hall or the coffee room. Bring to those meetings two copies—along with supporting exhibits—of a double-spaced report that doesn't run over two pages. Leave about a two-inch margin on the left for each of you to make notes. Be brief, but be thorough enough that he will not learn of some critical aspect of your performance later and from a third party.

Divide the written report and what you say into three parts: Progress (what you have done), Plans (what you want him to know about before you do it), and Proposals (things you need his permission to do and/or things only he can do). The next time it is your turn for a performance appraisal he should have few, if any, surprises to bring up. Further, you will have had a chance to do some research on those things that did surprise you when they came up during the review period.

Whenever the boss gives a positive or negative signal and includes some emotion with it, use your adult emotional state and become an active listener. It's a sure path to being able to influence him.

Patience Gains Acceptance by Associates

Installing a new communication system for performance interviews is difficult even if most of upper management is behind it. When you first introduce your style of communication into the appraisal or performance planning system, your veteran subordinates will be especially uncomfortable. Each of them has come to terms with this part of organizational life and will be suspicious of any change, no matter how attractive it may later prove. Some of those subordinates will come in convinced this is either another trip to the woodshed or another run of the perennial and general compliments. They will be ready for anything, but not for the kind of communication they will hear from you. They will come in determined to say as little as possible and will be surprised at your use of open-ended questions and your constructive reactions to their initially tentative responses.

Problems for You to Solve

The Great Stone Face

Under even the least stressful conditions Ted Argyllis didn't smile a lot and didn't frown a lot either. When he gave performance interviews the condition was aggravated. He never moved a facial muscle. During an interview the pitch and volume of his voice varied a little, but the pace was uniformly slow.

Ted's subordinates listened to the words a little but more to the monotone style of speech and saw the great stone face, as they called him. They were convinced he was angry with all of them and perhaps out to get them. Some of his subordinates complained to acquaintances in the human resources department, saying that Ted came into performance interviews ready to chew them up.

The HRD director went to Argyllis's boss, Bob Kallium, who was embarrassed about the whole thing. Kallium called Ted into his office and reminded him about his being named as a co-defendant in an equal employment lawsuit a few years back. Kallium knew the lawsuit had something to do with performance reviews, so he told Ted to change his attitude about them. This was the first time Kallium had mentioned the suit to Ted.

What Kallium didn't know was the Ted was trying to avoid playing favorites because he had been accused of that in the lawsuit. Ted thought the best thing to do was to avoid any smiles or other facial expressions that someone might interpret erroneously as negative or positive. As Ted sees it, he has a problem with his subordinates and another with his boss. He has come to you for advice.

"I'm a 'C' Student!"

My name is Benzoin, Dave Benzoin, but that doesn't matter. What does matter is that I just had my first performance appraisal and I was told in so many words that I am a "C" student! The hell I am! I had a 3.6 GPA at one of the toughest engineering schools in the country, which is a lot better record than that of any of the supervisors around here.

I'll admit to having loused up on a few design details, but that is not so unusual for a new engineer who had never seen some of the drawing practices they use around here. I did some good design work during the year, too, and I took the advice of a professor back in engineering school and arrived before eight and never left before five. So what happens? They have six categories on the form the supervisors use to write your appraisal record. The bottom one is so low it doesn't count. I was in the middle of the remaining five. In my book that's a "C."

The supervisor said something about a distribution of ratings and how first ratings vary a lot. Then he said I have a good future if I just keep up the quality of my design work. I'll give this outfit one more year.

Cross-References within This Book

Chapter 2 will remind you of the importance of the greeting ritual and small talk.

Chapter 3 will prepare you to seek a workable compromise as you and the appraisee jointly plan his and your future performance.

Chapter 4 will refresh your ability to listen for feelings as well as facts.

Chapter 5 provides a means of expressing your pleasure and your displeasure.

Chapter 6 warns you about nonverbal give-aways when you attempt to say one thing but feel another. It also sensitizes you to the nonverbal messages in the transmissions of the appraisee.

Chapter 7 emphasizes facts and feedback.

Chapter 8 describes the processes of even-handed presenting and informing the other party of the performance alternatives that are open to them and how to avoid the need to persuade.

Problems Solved

The Great Stone Face

Suggest to Ted that he tackle his problems one at a time. The first move is to make sure the HRD director has the facts on the lawsuit and knows the facts behind it. Next arrange a meeting with Kallium and the HRD director and review the facts. Whether Ted was guilty or not, point out to him that a lot of time has gone by and that his ability to give even-handed performance interviews is not under question.

The second problem will be a lot tougher. Start by convincing Ted to conduct a staged interview with a video camera on him. Next, suggest that he explore the importance of nonverbal communication in critical situations, such as performance interviews. Finally, have him practice developing more facial and vocal expression. This process will require a friendly and patient critic.

"I'm a 'C' Student!"

The supervisor let the appraisal form do some of his most critical communicating for him. And after Benzoin heard he was in the middle group he didn't hear anything else. What Benzoin didn't realize was that being a first-year engineer meant that the middle category rating in this firm was well over average, because they hired only engineers with high GPAs.

What the supervisor didn't realize was that Benzoin was accustomed to mostly "A" grades in a tough school, which meant he was far above average. The supervisor had followed the firm's instructions for filling out the form and had given it to Benzoin with little significant comment. If the supervisor does this again next year, Benzoin will either be on the job market or in a subtle form of early retirement.

References

Maier, Norman R. F. *The Appraisal Interview.* Wiley, New York, 1960.

12

The Communication Never Stops in Meetings

If you have never led a meeting of a group that hasn't worked together before or a group that is under extreme pressure, you will gain insight from this chapter into what to expect and how to respond constructively to whatever may occur. You will also learn how to live with the antics of such groups, to elicit the pertinent facts, and to join the group in fitting the facts into a productive result. More specifically, you will learn how to overcome the adverse effects of public, interpersonal conflict.

If you are a veteran of many meetings, you will be reminded that differences of opinion can be beneficial. You will also be reminded to learn to explore such differences without issuing personal challenges to others present. Said another way, you will learn to challenge ideas without attacking their sources.

You will increase your appreciation of the values of a decisionmaking discipline that can be used by a group.

Appraise the Situation

Nowhere in the working day of the engineer/manager are effective interpersonal communication skills more important than in meetings. The particular skills you will need will vary with the reason someone called the meeting in the first place. Those reasons can vary from "information only," through "it's Monday morning and it's the time," to "problem-solving," and even to "decisionmaking."

Whatever the announced purpose, if you are the leader, prepare yourself for some unpleasant surprises. Expect to encounter otherwise capable and helpful participants mentally checking out, fighting with others, attacking you, griping, avoiding blame at all costs, and nurturing a hidden agenda or two.

If this group hasn't worked together before or has been involved only in formal or one-way presentations, they will have to go through some developmental stages before becoming productive. Bruce Tuckman calls those stages forming, storming, norming, and performing. He derived those terms from observing the activities of groups in psychotherapy. Under "forming" he includes orientation to the ground rules, testing to establish interpersonal and task boundaries, and the establishment of dependency relationships with leaders and other group members. "Storming" is characterized by conflict and by polarization around interpersonal items, both of which act to prevent any progress on the task at hand.

"Norming" witnesses the development of a degree of group cohesiveness—putting aside differences, at least for the time being. Expressing personal options about the job becomes welcome, rather than taboo. In "performing," the roles of individuals become more flexible and personal pride subordinates to group accomplishment. Had Tuckman been observing groups of technically trained people he might have seen another stage. He might have seen the group members try, usually without lasting success, to move directly from forming to performing while submerging the interpersonal factors.

Although you might prefer different terms, think of those labels as memory aids to the steps of a process that can help you maintain your faith in the group. You might also prefer to add "nothing" as a phrase immediately preceding "storming" to reflect your experience with groups who waste valuable time studying the ceiling or doodling in their notepads. You may often wish that your group could avoid the storming phase. If they do, however, you won't like the results. If there is no storming, there will be no progress toward solving the human relations problems that always exist among members of a group.

You might wonder why you can't simply allow the group to go through the greeting ritual, spend some time in small talk, and then get down to business without having to worry about the nothing or storming phases. Here's a reason not to expect that easy progression: Just being in the presence of others can create stress in us. If the reason for being together is associated even indirectly with something that isn't as it should be, the stresses are multiplied. The resulting strains are obvious. For instance, have you ever noticed how the tone of voice and facial expression that an associate uses in a meeting are graphically different from what he uses in casual conversation?

Another source of stress is relative positions in the hierarchy. Some participants will arrive having convinced themselves that you, being a manager, already know what you want and will welcome only agreement. They have their own opinions; they don't know how you will react if your opinions are different, so they come to the meeting having decided that the best reaction is to take flight. They are primed to enter the "nothing" phase. By contrast, every now and then you will have a participant whose initial reaction is to fight and who will come ready to enter "storming."

Set the Objectives

It's too late to think about doing it all yourself. It's time to discipline your communication to help develop the group and its interactions. Make part of that development relate to the members learning to trust each other and to trust you.

Particularly if one or more of those present at the meeting reports to you, use your communication skills to help develop them as contributors in this and future meetings. That means helping them feel free to introduce pertinent facts when and where they fit, even if those facts are not complimentary to the interests or others in the meeting.

Communicate so as to encourage others to use their innate creativity to suggest causes for deviations from the plan (K-T Problem Analysis, see Chapter 10), and/or alternative actions to meet objectives (K-T Decision Analysis, see Chapter 10).

It is worthwhile to have as an objective communication that will make the next meeting more productive. It will be even more worthwhile if that objective is preceded by the objective of pursuing the present meeting to a productive conclusion. For example, if either the purpose or the progress of the meeting indicates an interest in some activity beyond that of the meeting, part of your job is to see that a follow-up system is agreed upon.

Select the Effective Mental State

If this is a group that has never tried to accomplish anything together, they are indeed forming. The enthusiasm possible to your positive natural-child ego state will serve the needs of the greeting ritual. Follow that with your critical-parent state as you engage in small talk.

If forming is followed by nothing, it's time for you, in your nurturing-parent role, to express common feelings, such as being nervous about what will happen next. If forming is followed by storming, avoid the critical parent and let the adult do some active listening to complaints or assertive coping with attempts to manipulate you. Then participate as the group sets some ground rules.

If this is a problem-solving or decisionmaking meeting, stay in the adult mode as you move into Kepner and Tregoe's situation appraisal.

By this time, the norming phase should have been replaced by performing. If it has not, there are some feelings that are acting as barriers to progress. It will take some adult active listening to be rid of them.

If you are concerned about how much time is available to the group, state your concern. Resist any temptation to move into your critical-parent role and threaten the rest with whatever dire consequences might result if they don't get on with it.

After the feelings are stated, stay in your adult state to help describe the problem. Let the others use their little-professor states for creativity in suggesting causes and alternatives, but be careful about using your little-professor state unless you have raised the trust levels to that place that the group will treat your ideas just as they do those of anyone else in the group.

The performing state includes the most intense and valuable communication. Anyone can question anybody about anything. The phase of time structuring that the group is in is trust. You are still the leader, but only for the purpose of accepting the blame from the next echelon up if the group fails.

Choose the Skills to Attain the Objectives

A training film, "Meeting in Progress" by Roundtable Films, illustrates most of the problems that engineer/managers encounter when they try to lead or even to participate in a problem-solving meeting. The film encourages meeting leaders to prepare for a meeting by sending out background data in advance to all likely attendees. Do it. In addition include an invitation for the participants to do some homework, such as gathering pertinent data and bringing copies of a summary of those data so that everyone can see it.

When the small talk is over, hand out a brief and easily read agenda. Have some extra copies of the background data for unexpected visitors or forgetful associates. You are ready for serious business. Don't count on the group's going through the forming and other stages, especially if they have worked together before, and don't try to force them into doing so.

Think of your function as the leader as fitting into the four-dimensional grid described in Chapter 1. The X axis includes all the things you do to influence the group to accomplish its mission. The Y axis includes those things you do to influence the group to work together productively and in harmony. The Z axis includes your own contributions to meeting the group's objective.

The significance of your being on a given axis is in the communication skills appropriate to it. Active listening fits on the Y axis. Self-disclosure and the coping skills of assertion belong on the Z axis. The factual aspects of the problem analysis and decision analysis of K-T are X-axis activities. Your previous experience may suggest that only the activities on the X axis are "truly management." Not so. Your communication obligations extend to all four axes.

Your encouragement to the members of the group to engage in ritual and small talk are Y-axis activities for you, the manager. Active listening and other things you do to help the members work out their emotions also belong on the Y axis.

Once you enter situation appraisal and ask for reactions to the information you sent out before the meeting, you are on the X axis. Use the manageable concerns from K-T to start, but don't call them that or mention K-T. If someone present has read the book, let them announce the connection, and then agree with them.

When you ask the group to agree on some rules, such as "Everyone seeks first to understand before trying to be understood," or "You can build on another's idea but you can't discredit it," you are on the X axis. Another way to state such protocols is like this: "Before anyone disagrees, he first states the opposing position to the satisfaction of its author, and without evaluating that position." Any guidelines for how the group will operate will mean much more if you set an example. That means displaying nonevaluative listening to feelings, careful listening to facts, and respecting the right of everyone present to express opinions and contribute facts.

If the situation appraisal leads you to problem analysis, asking for data, ways to express the deviation statement, and possible causes of the problem puts you on the X axis. When you stop during the meeting to summarize, clarify, or paraphrase what has already been said, you are still on the X axis.

Whenever you add your concerns to those of the others, you are on that leg of the Z axis that extends into the plane of the paper. You, the manager, are contributing to the group's work in your role as a competent professional. Your giving an opinion on the cause of a problem or a solution to it may risk polarizing opinion in the group, especially when the trust level is still on the low or uncertain side. When, however, you are technically qualified, and the group members know you are, run the risk. Anything short of that will do more to injure trust than will the polarization.

Part of your X-axis responsibilities is to obtain participation of everyone in the group according to their capability—not just to start them talking. Don't create some artificial standard that calls for approximately equal verbal contribution by everyone present. By the same token, if one or more of the group tends to dominate the conversation, don't treat him as if he were in his negative adaptive-child state. Interrupt him and summarize what he and others have contributed. Don't interrupt him and then call on someone else for an opinion. You will be failing in your obligations on the Y axis.

If you have never seen yourself on a video monitor, find a few objective critics and go through a mock meeting. Go through the tape carefully with two objectives. One is to modify your nonverbals to make them complement your words. The other is to check your abilities to sense which axis is best for the situation and what communication is appropriate for that axis.

Avoid the Risks Inherent with the Skills

The earlier you state your position or opinion, the more likely the group will attack it or decide their ideas aren't wanted. Trust hasn't had a chance to build, and you are still part of the "them" in the classical us-versus-them model of employees and their bosses. If you have any doubts of your status with the group, make your contributions in the form of two or more options of approximately equal accuracy or worth. In other words, choose to present rather than persuade.

You are likely to experience significant success in leading meetings using the techniques in this chapter. Some of your subordinates may attribute that success to your being such a good listener and leading without an obvious display of power. Their conclusion can lead them to trying to borrow some of your unused power and controlling part of the exercise. You may have to take a break and have a private discussion with such persons. The I message is ideal for expressing your position when that happens.

The Rewards

In simplest terms: project cost, project time, product cost, investment, and product quality. Not all those measures may be important in your organization, but all of them will accrue to you and your group. You will also obtain the reputation as a manager who can develop in his subordinates the ability to help a group work together to solve difficult problems.

Fit the Skills to Yourself and Your Job

Where do you sit in a meeting that you lead? If you sit at the head of a table that is longer one way than the other, why do you do it? If your answer to the second question is that you want everyone to know that you are the boss, you have chosen the right seat. If you want the meetings to be at least in part a means for you to exercise your power, you have chosen the right seat. If you have any other objective, you are in the wrong seat. You might consider sitting in the middle of one of the two long sides. The nonverbal translation is still that of power.

If you want a free flow of ideas and the trust of your reaction to those ideas without any contamination by your organizational position, sit on one of the long sides the next time you are in a meeting. But don't sit in the middle. If the layout doesn't lend itself to such variety, select your chair randomly, but don't crowd out someone who has a favorite location. If you find that a certain person always takes the seat opposite yours, you may be in a power contest. It's time for a private meeting and some active listening to find out what's behind it.

Who takes notes and then distributes the minutes? If you are not already doing it, pass the job to someone new each time you meet. Agree on when he will distribute the typed, double-spaced minutes and in what form.

How tight will the schedule be? The lower you think the trust level is between you and the rest, the more time you will need for the meeting. Further, whatever trust level you think you may have obtained, divide it in half. Trust in a boss is slow to build.

Just as when you are giving a presentation, when it is your turn to talk in the meeting, look briefly at, or in the direction of, everyone else. When one of them is speaking, look directly at that person until he finishes.

Patience Gains Acceptance by Associates

First, set an example of observing the dictate to show your recognition that everyone in every meeting is important and capable. Believe that, and it will show in your nonverbal signals; you won't have to mention it.

Evaluate your meeting-leading style by following up on any comment about your meetings. Do not assume in advance that a given comment is intended to be negative, no matter how awkwardly it may be expressed.

As soon as you feel that at least two of your subordinates are ready to practice the skills in this chapter, ask one of them to lead the next meeting. Then pass the job around. Now it's your turn to issue the minutes.

Problems for You to Solve

Invitation to Roller Derby

Billy Joe Township can't make it through a meeting without starting at least one brushfire. His boss, Stubnite, has landed on him several times, but to no avail. It isn't that Billy Joe tries to cause trouble; he just has a gift of finding a way to comment on someone else's idea that invariably provokes a fuss. If you were to read a transcript of the meeting, you might see nothing abrasive in his words. In fact, the same words would normally have no effect coming from someone else. Everyone in the group has had a taste of his technique, and none of them like it. Stubnite has asked you for some help.

My Turn

Doug Pobbs doesn't usually overwhelm the other engineers with talk. He can get wound up and run on a little, but most of the time he listens about as much as he talks. Put him in a meeting, though, and it's always his turn to talk. He will listen at first, but when the speaker mentions something with which Doug is familiar, he will break in and take off. He will never use ten words when thirty will do as well; his voice goes up about an octave from its usual pitch, and he doesn't stop for a breath until he has had his say. Aside from the often amazing display of lung capacity, Doug's comments are worthwhile but seldom earthshaking. He often interrupts the speaker without giving any indication that he recognizes what the speaker has been saying. None of the other engineers like his uninvited intrusions, but they usually consider the source and go on talking. Recently, however, one of them burst out with a serious attack on Doug and his interruptions. Doug needs help, knows it, and has come to you for some advise.

Cross-References within This Book

Chapter 2 will remind you of the importance of the greeting ritual and small talk.

Chapter 4 will refresh your ability to listen for feelings as well as facts.

Chapter 6 warns you about nonverbal give-aways when you attempt to say one thing but feel another. It also sensitizes you to the nonverbal messages in the transmissions of other-person appraisee.

Chapter 7 emphasizes facts and feedback.

Problems Solved

Invitation to the Roller Derby

By now part of the problem is Billy Joe's image with the rest of the group and with Stubnite. Even if he makes a 180–degree turnaround, many meetings will go by before the others will consider profiting by his comments. The odds are that Billy Joe is sending one or more non-verbal signals that cause irritation. It may be in his tone of voice or his facial expression, but one of those is irritating his listeners, probably by implying that the listener's ideas are inadequate.

My Turn

Doug changes when he goes into a meeting. It's not exactly a Jekyll and Hyde thing; it's more as if he has to prove himself. The more there is at stake, the more acute Doug is as a listener. Unfortunately, Doug listens solely for a cue that he sees as his ticket into the conversation. Then he not only speaks his piece but vents his nervous frustration by turning into motor mouth. People might overlook his habit when the group is still in small talk, but not when they are in problem-solving, especially when some of those present are nervous about some of the decisions that may have to be made.

There's no reason that Doug can't overcome his habit. The nervousness may not go away, but if he can learn the discipline of restating the other person's position before presenting his own, most of the adverse reaction to him will abate.

References

"Basic Tools" from *Communication Tools*, A Productivity Training Application Series, Control Data Business Advisors, Minneapolis, Minnesota, 1984.

Kepner, Charles H., and Benjamin B. Tregoe. *The New Rational Manager*. Kepner-Tregoe, Princeton, New Jersey, 1981.

Rogers, Carl R., and F. J. Roethlisberger. "Barriers and Gateways to Communication," *Harvard Business Review*, July-August, 1952.

Smith, Manuel J. *When I Say No, I Feel Guilty*. Bantam, New York, 1975.

Tuckman, Bruce W. "Developmental Sequence in Small Groups," *Psychological Bulletin*, Vol. 63, No. 6, 1965,, pp. 384–399.

"Meeting in Progress" by Roundtable Films, Beverly Hills, California, 1970.

13

Use the Telephone as If the Other Party Were in the Room

This chapter was written to influence you to use the phone just as if you were in the presence of the other party. There are suggestions about preparing to make an important call, making calls to potential clients whom you have never met, and the application of time structuring to phone conversations.

For those who are professional engineers in private practice, this chapter will help you make "cold" calls as part of your firm's business development program. You will discover the potential impact of the way in which you answer a call from someone outside the firm whom you have never met.

In spite of the telephone manners of the other party, you will be given alternatives to accepting his invitation to engage in roller derby.

This chapter suggests the wider use of nonverbals to increase your comfort level in any phone call.

Appraise the Situation

The most often-used channel of interpersonal business communication is the telephone. It is convenient and usually faster than in-person communication or the mail. Both of these attributes, however, can make the telephone a source of discomfort. For example, it can be an irritating interruption when you're trying to concentrate on something else. Telephones guilty of such transgressions have been thrown across rooms or had their cords yanked out of walls. Lasting damage to relationships have occurred because someone has used the wrong tone of voice over the phone.

On the other hand, the telephone is an invaluable adjunct to a business. The use of the phone to transmit data between computers is a separate subject, but data can also be transmitted between two or more people and recorded in the process.

Most technically trained managers whose firm offers a professional service dislike calling a stranger over the phone to ask about the possibility of work. The initial resistance to making "cold" phone calls may lie in its similarity to public speaking, which terrifies most of us. The longer-lasting dislike of cold calling may relate to the manager's fear of being rejected. This reluctance may seem strange in light of the superiority of cold calling over other means of developing market information. The cold call can produce valuable and timely information about contemplated contracts at little cost and in a short time. It can also provide a wealth of information about who in the prospective client's office is in charge of or knows about which project.

In addition to a reluctance to use the phone to collect valuable information, the phone conversations of many managers include such nonfluencies as "ah," "you-know," and "okay." Their grammar is full of mistakes. They are careless about their diction, which creates problems for their listeners. They use little voice inflection, variation of pitch, variation of volume, or anything that might be called animation.

They take long pauses without explanation or apparent reason. They take notes but often cannot decipher them later. They enter into complicated arrangements and agree to send a confirming memo but don't use feedback at the end of the conversation to clear up any misunderstanding.

They terminate a worthwhile call with only the briefest thank-you and say goodbye as if they were glad to be rid of the other person. They pass up a chance to reaffirm the relationship, which would make the next contact easier and more productive.

Some managers see any phone call as an unwelcome interruption. Their unspoken, "Don't bother me," and their animosity toward the caller are clear in their silences and tone of voice. They seem to believe they have no obligation to the caller unless he is a customer or the boss.

Other managers welcome phone calls, not as interruptions but because they provide an escape from whatever is going on at the moment. Their feeling of relief is apparent and seldom appropriate to the caller's purpose. In their relief, they disregard the unfortunate fact that all phone calls are or will be public information.

Set the Objectives

First, treat every caller as a client. In the broadest and most practical sense, a client is someone who has, is, or can benefit your organization or you personally.

Second, manage your phone communications, don't let them manage you.

Select the Effective Mental State

If you receive the call: Use your positive natural-child state and welcome a phone call as a chance to communicate with another human being. If the caller wants to spend some time in small talk, use your critical-parent state. If not, move into your adult state and stay there until the emotional problems have been solved and the technical and economic problems have at least been identified. When the business has been completed and the relationship between you and the caller is positive, switch to your natural-child state again and express your gratitude for the opportunity to work with him.

If you are the caller: Use the same mental states as you did when you received the call, except that the initiative to move into the adult state and start solving problems is yours.

Choose the Skills to Attain the Objectives

Do you remember the good old days when Ma Bell trained their operators and those of their more enlightened customers? "The voice with the smile wins" was one of their slogans. It made sense then; it still does.

When you have initiated the contact: Take the time to relax a minute or so before you make the call. Have your purpose clearly in mind or written. That purpose may be to obtain information, impart information, influence, or just make yourself feel better. Have paper and pencil ready for the vital stuff like names, projects, and dates. Place the call yourself! Make sure you won't be interrupted. An important call to a long-winded client could last over an hour.

Even if you don't take advantage of it to gesture, have a headset so you won't fumble around when you are trying to take notes. Don't use a tape recorder without the up-front permission of the other party, and don't use it then unless you have no choice. When people know they are being taped, they restrict their communication.

You are a guest in the other party's personal space. You may or may not have been invited. You may have intruded. You may even be unwelcome.

When you need information and have no idea for whom to ask, call the local chamber of commerce to learn the name of the chief executive. Dial the number well into the lunch hour. You will probably reach the receptionist or a secretary. Ask for the name of the person the receptionist thinks could help you. Write his name, title, and extension, and verify them in case the connection is broken or you have to call back later.

When you have reached the right person, briefly identify yourself and try to establish early rapport by making a remark that you intend as friendly. Mention something you and the prospect may have in common. If you feel awkward about making this call because the other party may be busy, say so, but don't apologize.

Assuming he doesn't hang up on you, here's another opportunity to practice time structuring. Couple your "hello" or "good morning" with a smile and the person's name (if you are sure you can pronounce it), and lift your chin a little in recognition, just as if he were standing a few feet from you. Simulate a hand shake? Normally no, unless you need the discipline to force yourself to observe time structuring.

Now for pastimes. Look at the imaginary person, not at your notes. If you can't think of anything better, look at a corner of the room or close your eyes. Do not look at anything that can distract you from the goal of small talk, which is to reduce the psychological distance between you and the other party.

Activities are next. If the other party signals that your call is unwelcome, it's time to borrow from assertion and use acknowledging. If he wants to explore the problem, it's time for negative assertion, manageable concerns, or negative inquiry. If he is emotional or disagrees with your position, it's time for active listening. Here again, act as if you were in his presence. Don't feel obliged to restart the conversation if he falls silent. Only when his emotions have run their course are you ready for the exchange of facts and workable compromise.

Once the facts start to flow, become a questioner and a listener. Phrase your questions so they start with who, what, where, why, when, and how. Stay away from can, are, will, did, have, could, has, does, and would, because they all steer the prospect toward a yes or no answer, and you won't learn as much. Limit your questions to your reason for calling.

When he starts to talk or respond, listen for ideas, not just words. Don't interrupt his speech or though processes. Concentrate, and don't worry if he is silent for awhile. Don't put words in his mouth. If you hear a negative signal, react to the signal, not to the person.

Lean slightly forward as you speak, just as you would if the two of you were in the same office. Smile as you speak (if it is appropriate). Vary the pitch and volume of your voice; cold calling is not for monotones. The lower the pitch of your voice, the more believable you will be.

Put some life into your words. Don't just pronounce words correctly, enunciate them so the hearer is sure of which of several similar-sounding words you just used. Choose some words that are common to your work and practice, saying them as a question, in surprise, with enthusiasm, and with pleasure.

Don't let the need to inject life cause you to speak so fast that the other party loses the thread. A good pace is about 130 words per minute. Use short pauses (a second or two) to avoid conveying coldness or lack of concern about your listener and to give you and the listener some time to think. A longer pause may make him wonder if the connection is broken or give the impression of pomposity or exaggeration.

Choose words that express, not impress, no matter how unimportant the other party's title may make you feel. Jargon is safe only after the other party has used it and you feel sure he is comfortable with it. The same goes, only more so, for technical terms. If you are a highly trained professional and find yourself resorting to esoteric terminology, chalk it up to your insecurity reflex and stop it.

When the activities are complete, wind down the conversation at about the pace you used to open it. Summarize the important facts and ask for confirmation. Your skill and determination to be sure of accurate feedback are even more important here than in face-to-face conversation.

After the feedback, express your appreciation, make a comment or two that is inconsequential (small talk) and say goodbye or an equivalent the same way you said hello.

Willing to practice? Even though you will be practicing your phone calling technique, use a video system. Have at least one critic and prepare him with a list of things you want him to listen and look for.

When you answer the phone: Every caller is a client, whether he works for your firm or a competitor. Therefore, make every phone call client-centered, which means communicating so the client will conclude you are trying to put yourself in his shoes and to meet his needs. No matter how angry the caller may be, at least he's talking at you and is giving you a chance to retain his business. You have no such chance with those who simply go elsewhere and gossip about your product or service.

The advice that held for the times when you initiated the call holds here, too. That includes animating your voice, obeying the practices of time structuring, and being an effective listener.

Avoid the Risks Inherent with the Skills

Your being a good telephone listener will inevitably catalyze those contacts who like to gossip. Don't participate! You have no idea who is listening or taping what you say.

Some clients who like to talk or who have no one else to listen to them without telling them what to do will consume your time just as they would if they were in your group.

The Rewards

Cold phone calls pay large dividends for those whose livelihood depends on projects awarded by customer groups. The cold call can produce valuable and timely information about contemplated contracts at little cost and in a short time. It can also provide a wealth of information about who in the prospective client's office is in charge of or knows about what project.

Observing even the basic rules of telephone etiquette can lead you to otherwise reluctantly offered information. Practicing active listening, even over the phone, can develop still more significant information. Disciplined listening and asking for confirmation of feedback can also help you make fewer errors when you act on the basis of a telephone call.

Allowing a conversation to progress from a friendly hello into small talk before trying to direct the other party's attention to the business purposes of a call can develop a personal rapport between you and the other party, even though you never have seen each other. You will discover mutual areas of interest and may look forward to the pastimes part of the next conversation you have with this person.

Fit the Skills to Yourself and Your Job

Admit your need for help in making better use of the phone, seek it, and accept it when offered. Some of the people with whom you converse regularly will be glad to give you some tips. Some of them may have seen videotapes on the proper use of the phone and will enjoy talking about them.

Patience Gains Acceptance by Associates

Your biggest problem in changing your own habits may be the habits of others. They use the phone all the time but have never taken the trouble to evaluate how they do it. Evaluating your telephone communication and making changes will make you stand out and may make you feel self-conscious. As part of the changes you want to make, prepare a few answers to the question, "What are you trying to do?"

Problems for You to Solve

Mumbles

Bud Dubbes can speak plainly under most conditions. One of those conditions, however, is not the phone, especially when he has to call a municipal utility board to ask about upcoming engineering contracts. Bud works for a consulting firm of architects and engineers, and his technological and leadership abilities are beyond question, but his future will be limited until he learns how to make cold calls.

He breaks out in a cold sweat; his normally baritone voice escalates to that of a lyric tenor, and he mumbles his first few words. The people he calls in prospective client organizations sometimes have patience with him and just wait until he can get into the meat of the call. Once he does, he is okay. Not all client representatives are so forgiving, though. In fact, one called a principal of Bud's firm and complained about Bud's wasting his time. Bud has come to you because of your experience in communication. He has ambitions, but he realizes that his inability to talk on the phone with important strangers is hurting him.

It's Not Our Problem

Mark Sullefit is vice president of engineering in a large manufacturing firm. He has been in this job almost ten years. He earned his promotion by hard work, good engineering, and knowing how to communicate with the accountants in the controller's office about budgets and project payoffs. Since being in the office, he has earned a reputation for direct, often blunt communication with marketing and vendors. He realizes the need for occasional contacts with customers but sees customer relations as the responsibility of the marketing people.

Customer representatives hate to call engineering. They have complained about being left hanging by engineers who don't sound as if they have any real obligation to solve a customer's problem and secretaries who are carefully noncommittal.

The vice president of marketing is George Pyrofax. He has heard many complaints from customers about the communication with engineering. George has been with the company only two years and is not too sure of his role. He has talked with Tom Harmington, the executive vice president, about the problem, but Tom is reluctant to confront anyone, especially Sullefit. Tom is about ready to retire and doesn't want to participate in any more corporate battles. The president, who used to be the financial vice president, travels to New York a lot and still keeps his contacts in the financial world. His knowledge of engineering is limited to its cost, the difficulty in communicating with its people, and its necessity to the business.

Cross-References within This Book

Chapters 3, 4, and 7 contain material that is directly useful in phone conversation.

Chapter 5 covers the techniques of confrontation, which will not be as effective over the phone as they are intended to be when you and the other person can see each other. Coupling the phone with slow-scan television allows more nonverbal exchanges, but they are not sufficient for direct criticism and compliments.

Problems Solved

Mumbles

As far as Bud is concerned, calling a total stranger and engaging him in conversation designed first to establish a personal rapport is a lot like public speaking. Bud hates public speaking. For him to have to proceed with the conversation to unearth and qualify the possibilities of some project for the office is unbearable. The fact that he does a good job once he is over the first hurdle suggests the problem is not insolvable.

The first part of the answer to Bud's problem is for him to practice with someone who will not help him over the starting hurdle. The second part is developing the words and nonverbals of an effective opening statement and memorizing both until he can "set it on automatic" for the first minute or so. Later, when his confidence builds, he can be more flexible. The third part is for the critic to reinforce whatever Bud does well, as soon as he does it. One more thing: most people need practice in their telephone diction. Make sure Bud receives some.

It's Not Our Problem

The ball is in George Pyrofax's court. He won't achieve anything by complaining to the executive vice president, and the president's mind is on finance. George's most likely route to success is to find a couple of engineers who are doing a good job on the phone, then to solicit a customer's help in quantifying what makes a good performance on the phone. Next is to compliment those engineers through Sullefit, with emphasis on the value of quality use of the telephone.

Sullefit will be suspicious at first and will react cautiously to George's overtures. If, however, George has practiced his active listening and assertive coping skills, he will be able to cultivate a more productive relationship with Sullefit. Toward the end of that conversation he can switch to "present and inform" and outline the benefits and internal changes needed to enlist the engineers in helping with customer relations. The tricky part will be for George to avoid communicating from his parent ego state and blaming Sullefit for the problem. The successful conclusion will include Sullefit's admitting his people do have a responsibility to the customer beyond designing quality products.

References

Connor, Richard A., Jr., and Jeffrey P. Davidson. *Marketing Your Consulting and Professional Services*. Wiley, New York, 1985.

Jones, Gerre L. *How to Market Professional Design Services*, 2d ed. McGraw-Hill, New York, 1983.

14

Epilogue: Why Have We Taken So Long?

All of the skills advocated in this book and their benefits to practitioners have been known for years. But why aren't they more widely used? The guiding philosophy of interpersonal relations—"Love thy neighbor"—was suggested at least 2500 years ago, but why haven't we summoned the courage to try it on a broad scale? Why haven't we used it more widely in management, especially since it offers a route to greater productivity?

Is it because the teaching of these skills has become the province of churches, consultants, and colleges but not corporations? Is it because we treat interpersonal communication as we do everything else of significance and say that it must start with top management? (And top management never heard of it or doesn't see the payoff?)

Does it have to start in the home? If it does, the handicap is enormous. Aside from communication skills, we are a long way from teaching basic parenting to most parents. Thomas Gordon wrote two books, *Parent Effectiveness Training* and *PET Revisited*, that are addressed to parents and contain much of the material in this book. But their initial popularity has waned.

Is all this the responsibility of higher education? The colleges teach ethics and interpersonal communication, but the engineers look down on them as "pud" courses and take them only to satisfy part of the humanities requirements for their degree. Medical, dental, and law students often take communications courses, but not the one that could help them mange. Business school curricula have courses on human behavior, but an emphasis on interpersonal communication is hard to detect.

The result: The courses that could be of great value to those who will eventually manage projects are taken primarily by students in the humanities—a curious inconsistency when you realize that liberal arts students generally start by being better at communication than are their technically trained counterparts. Are we educating the wrong part of the population? Or are we promoting people with the wrong degrees?

Another problem: The faculties in the professional curricula are much better at lecturing and publishing papers on interpersonal relations than at living them. Students learn by reading, taking notes, reciting, and passing examinations, but seldom by example. Publishing and obtaining grants constitute success in academe, not re-orienting the mental states of students to prepare them for intensive communication with their associates-to-be in stressful, organizational settings.

Even if we did teach interpersonal skills to engineering, law, medical, dental, and business students, would they benefit from something that is intended for the world of management? As undergraduates they have almost no concept of being the boss or a member of a project team, or of communicating with a boss. Those students stand a better chance of developing their interpersonal communication skills after they have been on the job for a few years and are ready for promotion. So, shall we leave it to continuing education and consultants to put it all together?

The broad acceptance of the philosophy of "Love thy neighbor" is yet to come in for-profit organizations. Is it possible we just don't know how? If that is the problem, the interpersonal communication skills in this book provide an answer. They have been presented as a means of putting that philosophy to work. Will you use them to that end?

Glossary

Acknowledgement
An alternative to Fogging, a term introduced by Manuel J. Smith. It means recognizing but neither arguing nor agreeing with someone who has accused you incorrectly of doing something wrong.

Activities
Taken from TA, it is one of the six ways we structure our communicating time. Ideally, it follows Pastimes. It is what we are primarily expected to do as managers. It includes making decisions and solving problems relative to technical, economic and interpersonal matters.

Adaptive Child State
One of the ego states or metal attitudes that go to make up TA. It is the one from which we communicate according to what we learned as children as means of coping with the pressures of our parents and other authority figures.

Adult State
This is the TA ego state from which we communicate our logic and rational thought. It is primarily used to exchange views with someone else who is also in his Adult.

Authenticity
This is the rarest of the ways in which we structure our communicating time. It is the result of our and another person's having learned to trust each other implicitly. It is also called intimacy and honesty.

Body Language	All of our movements (or lack of movement) from the tops of our heads to the tips of our toes send messages. Included are the other things that people can see when they look at us, such as the clothes we wear, our hair style, our facial hair, and our fingernails.
Broken Record	Another part of Manuel J. Smith's techniques of assertion, it means calmly repeating your wishes without allowing your emotions to interfere and continuing to do so until the other person recognizes your position, or the two of you start seeking a compromise.
Confrontation	The technique of communication that can effectively present your position when someone else has done something that has affected your emotions and your job, either positively or negatively. Thomas Gordon's "I Message" offers a basis for the communication.
Coping	Children Cope with parental attempts to exert authority, sometimes by obeying but more often by less productive behavior.
Critical Parent State	When persons in positions of authority feel they must discharge their obligation to control, discipline, or punish their subordinates, they communicate from this ego state.
Decision Analysis	One of the four techniques that Kepner and Tregoe propose, this one starts with stating what is to be resolved and ends with considering what might go wrong with the preferred course of action.
Ego State	Part of the theory of TA is that each of our communications issues from one of several "persons" within us and is directed toward one of the persons that make up the other party to the discussion. An analysis of our communications discloses that we send messages from our Critical Parent, Nurturing Parent, Adult, Adaptive Child, Natural Child, and Little Professor.
Empathy	Occurs when you can share someone else's feelings or ideas without letting it affect your judgment.

Feedback	Invited: You send a message to someone and then ask him to tell you in return what he thinks you were trying to say.
	Uninvited: Someone shows by his communication that something is affecting his emotions and actions. You tell him what you understand his situation to be (see Active Listening).
Fight	Used in this book to include all the aggressive behaviors and communications that result from stress from someone else's actions.
Flight	Includes all the passive behaviors and communications that result from stress from someone else's actions.
Fogging	One of the techniques of assertion that helps you avoid manipulation by someone else without fighting or fleeing (see Acknowledging).
Forming	Bruce Tuckman proposes this as the first step of a group meeting with the objective of solving problems. It includes orientation, marking off territories, and the establishment of dependency relationships. For a group to attain their ultimate in problem-solving it will be followed by Storming.
Free Information	Manuel Smith urges us, as part of being assertive, to listen more carefully to what the other party says. The result may be our learning something about the topic or about the speaker. What we learn is free because we neither have to ask for it nor give something in return.
Games	Another of the six ways in which we structure our communicating time, this one gathers all the negatives that we use to injure others. It includes snide remarks, putdowns, and insults. More than half the communication within an organization fits under games.
I Message	Proposed by Thomas Gordon as a three-component means of expressing the emotional and factual effects of someone else's action upon you. The concept recognizes that the person whose situation

has been affected by another's actions "owns the problem." The problem-owner's interests will be served best by defining his situation but not by attacking the other party nor by ignoring the incident.

Inform
The unbiased offering of information to another person as part of your presentation. The other party is then free to choose among the several courses of action that you present.

Intimacy
The pinnacle condition of time structuring (see Authenticity).

Little Professor State
The part of our communication with which we express our creativity. It may be intended to injure or to help.

Manageable Concerns
Part of Kepner and Tregoe's situation appraisal—the things that concern us and are within our ability to control or at least affect. Fits well into Manuel Smith's system of assertiveness.

Musts
Part of Kepner and Tregoe's decision analysis is the setting of objectives before deciding on a course of action. At least one of those objectives is an essential result. It qualifies as a Must if it can be measured.

Natural Child State
This is the part of us from which we communicate our emotions, whether positive or negative. Much of the time we are unable to control it.

Negative Assertion
Another one of the ways of avoiding manipulation by someone who is determined to capitalize on an error you have made. You admit the error, say how you feel about it, and stop. You neither argue nor apologize (see Acknowledging).

Negative Inquiry
Another way of avoiding manipulation by someone who is determined to capitalize on something you did. You ask what is wrong with the action and continue to ask until the other party comes out with a reason that you see as basic and resolvable.

Norming
That stage in the development of a work group in which it becomes okay to state personal opinions about the job.

Nurturing Parent State
One of the ego states of TA, this one issues our communications that are intended to

	protect, rescue, or take over from another party whose ability we see as inadequate to the task.
Open-ended Question	Any question that cannot be answered by a yes or no and that invites a free expression of opinion. Master the ability to ask Open-ended Questions before you try to obtain Invited Feedback (see Feedback, Invited). May be called "open question."
Parent State	The combination of Critical and Nurturing Parent that contains all we have learned to communicate by contact with our parents and authority figures.
Pastimes	One of the six ways we structure communicating time. It is sometimes referred to as small talk or chit chat. It is a time for patience and agreement but not for solving problems. The participants are most effective if they are communicating from one of their parent ego states. Ideally, it starts after Ritual and precedes Activities.
Performing	Bruce Tuckman calls this the time of group accomplishment.
Persuade	One of the two basic objectives of factual communication in an organization. See Present for the other. The idea is to communicate in such a way that the other person changes what he does or says. It includes direct, convince, and order.
Present	The other of the two basic objectives of factual communication in an organization. The idea is to communicate in such a way that the other person can make an objective choice among the courses of action you have presented.
Problem Analysis	One of the four techniques that Kepner and Tregoe propose, this one starts with stating a deviation from the expected and ends with a probable underlying cause.
Ritual	One of the six forms in which we structure our communicating time. It includes the words and gestures associated with seeing someone after a separation and breaks the

	silence of Withdrawal. Ideally, it is followed by Pastimes.
Roller Derby	The term Dru Scott gave to the typical organizational communication environment. Everyone goes around the oval, gives and receives occasional bruises, puts on a great show, and accomplishes little or nothing.
Small Talk	See Pastimes.
Storming	Bruce Tuckman proposes this as the second step of a group meeting with the objective of solving problems. It includes conflict and polarization around interpersonal items. Ideally, it is followed by Norming.
Stroke	Any signal from one person that can be sensed by the recipient. It may be words, sounds, smells, sights, or touches. It may be injurious, helpful, or neutral.
TA	Transactional Analysis.
Time Structuring	That part of TA that classifies our communications into Withdrawal, Ritual, Pastimes, Activities, Authenticity, and Games (see these entries).
Transaction	When one person directs a Stroke at another (a stimulus) and the other person gives one in return (response), the two of them have shared a Transaction.
Transactional Analysis	A theory of human communication that began with Eric Berne's observations on the things his patients did to elicit Strokes from someone else.
Wants	Part of Kepner and Tregoe's decision analysis is the setting of objectives before deciding on a course of action. The Want objectives are not essential but have different degrees of desirability.
Withdrawal	One of the six forms in which we structure our communicating time. In it, however, we are neither sending nor receiving Strokes form another person. Ideally, is followed by Ritual when we encounter someone.
Workable Compromise	The primary objective of the assertive techniques taught by Manuel Smith. In it two parties agree on a course of action or a division of the property but without the requirement of fairness or equal division.

You Messages

Gordon points out that those of us who have not been trained in the use of I Messages will usually devote their communication to accusing the offending party. The accusations start with "You" . . . and go on to emphasize the transgression and often to threaten retaliation or punishment.

Index

About the Author

DALE E. JACKSON is Director of the Engineering Management Graduate Program, School of Engineering, University of Kansas. He has led workshops on leadership and interpersonal communication, written communication, supervisory skills, and engineering management. The author of *Cost Engineering Analysis,* he holds two major U.S. chemical patents.